Fundamentals of Course Analysis
for Agility Handlers

Written by Stuart Mah

17 Industrial Dr., South Hadley, MA 01075

For more information contact:

Clean Run Productions, LLC
17 Industrial Dr.
South Hadley, MA 01075
Phone: (413) 532-1389 or (800) 311-6503
Fax: (866) 758-6503
Website: www.cleanrun.com

Edited by Nini Bloch, Monica Percival, Marcille Ripperton, Lisa Baird, and Betsey Lynch
Cover Photo by JT pawPrints
Book Design and Typesetting by Robin Nuttall
Cover Design by Robin Nuttall

ISBN 1-892694-10-7

To my wife and best friend Pati.
Thanks for being there. You are the one.

And to Qwik, Alley, Jet, Recce, Gracie, Lilly, and Cane.
All of you continue to teach me more than I teach you.

Table of Contents

Acknowledgments vii

About the Author ix

Introduction xi

Chapter 1: Jumps and Jumping Patterns **13**
    Serpentine 13
    Threadle 14
    Pinwheel 14
    270° Turn 15
    180° Turn 16
    Right Angle Turn 17
    Offset Line 18
    Slicing 19
    Problems with Jump Types 20

Chapter 2: Challenges **21**
    Obstacle Discriminations 21
    Options 24
    Handler Restrictions 26
    Directional Discriminations 29
    Spacing Problems 30
    Approaches 32

Chapter 3: Handling Maneuvers **33**
    Rear Cross 34
    Front Cross 35
    Blind Cross 37
    Counter Rotation 38
    Reverse Flow Pivot 38
    V-Set 40
    Lead-Out Advantage 43
    A Heirarchy of Cues 46

Chapter 4: Directional Cues **49**
    Go On 49
    Get Out 49

Chapter 5: The Concept of Leads **53**

Chapter 6: Concepts of Course Analysis **59**
    Study the Course Beforehand 59
    Look at the Course from the Dog's Point of View 59
    Draw the Handler's Path 60
    Think of a Course in Terms of Sequences 61
    Practice the Course in the Walk-Through 62

Chapter 7: Course Analysis Practice **63**

Chapter 8: Putting it All Together **93**

Acknowledgments

An author cannot write any type of text without somebody helping to make the text not only readable, but also understandable. That is the job of the editor. If the editor does the job as required, the result is a book. If the editor does the job well, the text not only becomes readable, but it is improved well beyond the original text into something more than a book. The book essentially becomes an extension of the author. The credit for this goes to Nini Bloch, whose numerous hours of reading and editing have made this book something more.

This is the second in the series of books for Clean Run so thanks also also go to Monica Percival and Clean Run for taking the time to print and publish this book.

Finally, thanks go to all the people who were good enough to purchase the first book in this series, *Fundamentals of Course Design for Dog Agility,* and provided the encouragement for me to write a second book. It is my sincere hope that both books provide the agility handler, from novice to expert, with a basis for course analysis and lead to more successful and enjoyable runs.

Stuart Mah with his dog Qwik in the 2003 USDAA Steeplechase Finals. Photo by Joe Canova

About the Author

Inspired by Kathy Lofthouse to begin agility, Stuart Mah became active in the sport in 1989. The rest is history. His first agility dog All-American Shannon was selected as a member of the first U.S. Agility Team ever assembled for international agility competition. That team traveled to Germany in 1991 and captured a bronze placement in the premier of the Agility World Cup competition. In 1992, Stuart and Shannon once again competed on the U.S. Agility Team in the Agility World Cup in Spain. In addition, Shannon competed in the United States Dog Agility Association (USDAA) National Finals four times, earning a win in 1991 and two bronze placements in 1993 and 1994. Shannon was also a member of the three-dog team that won the National Dog Agility Masters tournament in 1991 and was elected to the USDAA Agility Hall of Fame that year. Shannon retired after attaining her Agility Dog Champion (ADCH) title in 1995 at the age of 10 years.

Stuart's first Border Collie, Recce, was the top dog in the nation in the 30" jump height division in 1994 and earned a top-four placement in the 1994 USDAA Grand Prix National Finals. Recce attained his ADCH in 1995 at the same trial that Shannon did. In addition, Stuart and Recce were members of the 1995 U.S. Agility Team that competed in Belgium. In 1996, this dynamic duo was selected by the AKC as members of the first U.S. team ever assembled to participate in the World Agility Championships, held in Switzerland. In 1998, Recce won the 24" AKC Agility Championship. Recce earned his AKC MACH and his USDAA APD titles and retired last year from agility.

Qwik, a 4-year-old Border Collie (opposite), went from first time in the ring to ADCH in a year, placed in the 2003 USDAA Steeplechase finals, and finished second in the 2003 USDAA Grand Prix. He has also appeared in the Purina Incredible Dog Challenge and the ESPN Outdoor Games. Alley Cat, a 6-year-old Pembroke Welsh Corgi, finished her ADCH last year and made it to the semifinals in the Grand Prix.

Currently, Stuart runs Rising Stars Dog Agility in Florida with his wife, Pati Hatfield Mah. Their students have gained top honors in national competition and earned agility titles in all flavors of the sport. Six of their students have become national champions, and one was the only "triple crown" winner (AKC, NADAC, and USDAA national wins in the same year) in agility history. Stuart has judged for all major U.S. agility organizations as well as internationally. He has written articles for the USDAA *Dog Agility Report*, *Southern California Dog Magazine*, and *Clean Run*, and was voted "Agility Person of the Year" in 1996 by the USDAA.

Introduction

This is the second in a series of books about course design for dog agility. I wrote the first book, *Fundamentals of Course Design for Dog Agility*, to help new as well as experienced judges gain insight into the causes and effects of course design. This book addresses the topic of standard agility courses from the perspective of the handler. It is an attempt to bridge the gap between what judges design and expect from a course, and what we as handlers should or would like to attempt to create the best run possible.

Included in this book are definitions of agility terms. Any technical or complex sport has its set of terms used to describe elements that are unique to that sport. Often the term doesn't even begin to describe the reality. "Shotgun formation," for example, isn't a bunch of duck hunters on parade but a specific offensive pass setup in American football. The same gap between the jargon and the reality applies to agility. The following chapters include descriptions of course setups or handling maneuvers that an agility handler needs to know to understand the course analysis descriptions. In certain cases, a particular maneuver is known by more than one term. In these cases, I've used the most commonly accepted term although I've mentioned the alternative where applicable.

The chapter on leads and lead shifts explains many of the reasons why a dog moves through the course the way he does.

My comments are gleaned from the observation of thousands of handlers and dogs running courses of my design. They are also based on the observation of handlers and dogs running the same courses that I have attempted with my own dogs. I hope that with this current volume I can give both new and experienced handlers better insight into making the correct handling choices for their dogs.

Stuart Mah

Bryceville, Florida

1 Jumps and Jumping Patterns

In describing a course, handlers and instructors often use a kind of "agility shorthand" to characterize specific patterns of obstacles, especially the way jumps are arranged on a course. For example, instead of saying, "Take the first jump by slicing it to the left, the second by slicing it to the right, and the third jump by slicing it to the left," if the pattern of jumps fits, we can simply say, "do a serpentine." This shorthand is succinct and descriptive of the dog's path through the jump pattern. What follows is a description of some of the more common jump patterns. Also, where applicable, the explanation will describe the ideal way to perform the pattern.

Serpentine

A serpentine is an arrangement of jumps, as in **Figure 1-1,** such that the dog must snake or *serpentine* through the sequence. Most frequently consisting of three jumps, a serpentine occasionally includes four or five jumps. To jump efficiently through a serpentine, the dog must adjust his angle of approach or turn rate so that he can take the shortest, straightest path between jumps, which may be difficult. The wider the dog's arc, the greater distance he will run and the slower his time will be. In addition, the dog will spend more time looking for the next jump because the next jump will always be behind and far to the side of the dog rather than in front and slightly offset, as shown in **Figure 1-2.** While some handlers argue that the more efficient path can lead to more dropped bars, in actuality it creates fewer bar problems since the dog doesn't have to change direction so radically at every jump. The most common course fault in this setup is a refusal.

Figure 1-1. A typical three-jump serpentine pattern requires that the dog adjust his approach angle so that he can take the shortest, straightest path.

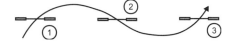

Figure 1-2. An efficient serpentine path (solid line) is shorter and less loopy than an inefficient one (dotted line) and places obstacles in front of rather than behind and far to the side of the dog.

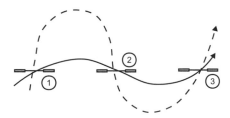

Threadle

Figure 1-3. A handler needs to have good control of his dog to execute a threadle. Faults— typically off-courses, refusals, and dropped bars—are much more common than with a serpentine.

Similar in arrangement to the serpentine, the threadle differs in that all the jumps must be taken in the same direction, as shown in **Figure 1-3**. This maneuver is much harder to perform since the handler needs to keep a much closer rein on the dog to bring him through the gap between jumps. Failure to do so will result in a dog taking a jump in the wrong direction (*backjumping*). In addition, because of the shortened distance to the next jump, the dog must be able to set up for the jump more quickly and often must change directions at the same time. The most common course faults with the threadle setup are off-courses, followed by refusals and displaced bars.

Pinwheel

Figure 1-4. A pinwheel challenges the dog with a circle of jumps arranged like the spokes of a wheel.

The pinwheel setup shown in **Figure 1-4** features jumps arranged in a circular fashion similar to the spokes of a wheel. Usually a pinwheel consists of three jumps, but it may consist of four. The jumps are usually spaced evenly around an axis. One challenge with pinwheels is that if a dog jumps long over one jump as in **Figure 1-5A**, he may run around the next jump, especially if it is a less visible nonwinged jump. If the course heads in another direction immediately after the pinwheel, as in **Figure 1-5B,** the pinwheel's arc will aim the dog in the wrong direction and tempt him to take the wrong obstacle. Consequently, in pinwheels, the handler must be more certain which way his dog is facing each jump. Otherwise, if the handler moves prematurely, he can send the dog over the wrong obstacle.

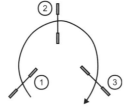

Figure 1-5. A dog that jumps long over one jump in a pinwheel as in A risks a runout at the next jump. In the pinwheel in B, #6 aims the dog toward the wrong jump. The handler cannot start to move out of the pinwheel until his dog has finished turning to the correct jump.

270° Turn

From the handler's point of view, a 270° turn is a jump pattern in which the angle from one jump to the other is 270°, as in **Figure 1-6**. The appearance is similar to a pinwheel with the center jump missing. For a judge, a 270 describes the path of the dog as he moves through the pattern, as shown in **Figure 1-7A**. Here the dog must actually turn 270° in from the teeter to the A-frame, so this turn is known as a *true 270*. In **Figure 1-7B**, although the jumps are arranged exactly as in the first case, the dog actually only turns 180°, so this turn is known as a *pseudo-270*.

Figure 1-6. A 270° turn resembles a pinwheel without the center spoke.

Figure 1-7. In A, the dog executes a true 270, turning a full 270° from the teeter to the A-frame. Despite the jump arrangement in B, the dog only turns 180° from the teeter to the A-frame, executing a pseudo-270.

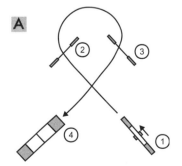

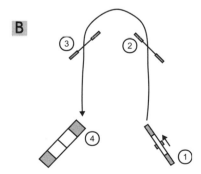

180° Turn

A 180° turn is an arrangement of obstacles in which the dog turns 180° from one obstacle to another. When referring to jumps, the pattern seen most often is similar to a two-jump serpentine, as in **Figure 1-8.** This setup is sometimes known as a *blind 180* since the dog has no obstacle to focus on when turning back to the second jump. One variation on this turn is a *push-out 180*, where the next jump is in front and to the side of the first jump, as in **Figure 1-9**. In this case, the dog must go out and around to pick up the correct side of the second jump. Taking the second jump in the wrong direction (backjumping) is the most common fault since it makes more sense to the dog to move right and take the jump, as in **Figure 1-10,** than to go by and around it to approach it from the opposite direction. Another variation is the *drop-back 180* turn in **Figure 1-11**. In this case the dog not only has to turn 180° but also has to move back past the first jump to find the next jump. With the drop-back 180, the dog has to work hard to find the second jump. The most common errors are incurring a refusal by running around the second jump or arcing wider than normal to the second jump, as shown in **Figure 1-12.** A fast dog often turns so wide that he misses the jump entirely.

Figure 1-8. In a typical 180° turn, the dog must reverse direction.

Figure 1-9. A push-out 180 turn requires the dog to go beyond the second jump and turn back 180° to jump it.

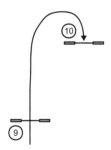

Figure 1-10. Backjumping the second jump is a common problem with push-out 180 turns.

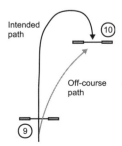

Figure 1-11. A drop-back 180 turn requires the dog to turn back 180° to find the second jump behind the first.

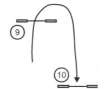

Figure 1-12. Turning wide and missing the second jump is a common problem with a drop-back 180 turn.

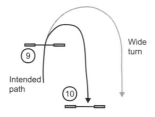

Right Angle Turn

Also known as a 90° turn, the right-angle turn comes in three types. The *true 90* presents an even, smooth turn, as shown in **Figure 1-13.** The second and third types of right-angle turns are known as *depressed angle turns* because, in both cases, the second jump is set up in such a way as to require a more acute, or tighter, turn from the dog.

Figure 1-13. In a true right-angle or 90° turn, the dog's arc is smooth and symmetrical.

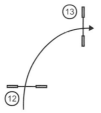

In the *push-out 90* turn shown in **Figure 1-14**, the second jump is positioned much farther away from the first jump than in the true 90. In performing this turn, the dog has to drive out to the second jump and then turn smartly, with relatively little room to maneuver. The most common problem with this setup is for the dog to turn too sharply, resulting in a refusal as the dog misses the jump to the inside. In the *drop-back 90*, shown in **Figure 1-15**, the dog needs to turn quickly right off the bat. Again, the most common course fault for this setup is a refusal because the dog ends up on the outside of the jump rather than on the inside as with a push-out turn.

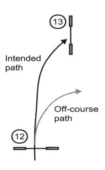

Figure 1-14. In a push-out right-angle turn, the dog must push out to the second (depressed) jump, turning abruptly at the end of the arc. Failure to do so will result in a refusal to the inside of the second jump.

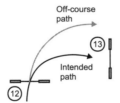

Figure 1-15. In the drop-back right-angle turn, the dog needs to pivot faster in the first part of the turn or he'll earn a refusal to the outside of the second jump.

Offset Line

A line of jumps as in **Figure 1-16,** in which the path is not completely straight but staggered or *offset*, is called an offset line. If a dog fails to see the stagger and focuses instead on the assumed "straight line" of jumps, a refusal is almost certain, with an off-course frequently following.

Figure 1-16. Refusals and off-courses are common on an offset line of jumps such as this one, where the dog may focus on the line between #2 and #4, failing to see jump #3.

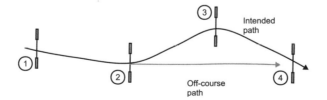

Slicing

When a dog takes an approach to a jump that sends him at an angle, as in **Figure 1-17**, rather than directly perpendicular to the jump bar, he is *slicing* the jump. This maneuver can be an efficient way to shorten distance between jumps on a curve since it reduces the dog's turning radius after landing. The problem this strategy presents is that since the dog is jumping a proportionally wider amount of bar, as shown in **Figure 1-18**, he will need to stay tucked up longer and hence land farther away from the jump. Thus, when a dog slices a jump at a severe angle, he may land as far away from the jump as if he had just taken a spread jump—the more severe the slice, the longer the landing distance away from the jump. If the dog needs to take a tight turn immediately after the jump, especially away from the handler, he can get into trouble. To accommodate the turn, the dog may drop his rear end early and knock a bar during the direction change.

Figure 1-17. When a dog slices a jump instead of taking it straight-on, his body passes over the bar at an angle.

Figure 1-18. Whatever the angle, when the dog slices a jump, it will increase the depth of the jump making it equivalent to performing a spread jump. In A, the dog goes straight over the bar so that his body is passing over a very narrow area of the jump bar. In B, the dog is slicing the jump, which causes him to jump a proportionally wider area of the bar, making it equivalent to performing a spread jump.

Problems with Jump Types

One final consideration is to examine the types of hurdles that a dog is asked to jump. For example, the typical agility jump consists of a 4'- to 5'-long bar, typically with a 2'-wide wing attached to each standard, so the total expanse of the jump is between 8' and 10'. This obstacle is usually easy for even the most novice dogs to see—an advantage on course, especially where an angle of approach is acute. The wings help give the dog a reference point. If a handler needs to run close to his dog to get him to take a jump, however, a wing can force the handler away from the bar, and, if the dog follows the handler, the dog will run around the jump. By contrast, a nonwinged jump, while easier to negotiate for a handler who must stay in tight to his dog, becomes harder for the dog to see the more acute his angle of approach gets. Furthermore, if a dog turns away, then turns back to an angled, nonwinged jump, it becomes easier for the dog to miss and run around the jump.

In jumping spreads, the dog not only needs to cover height but depth as well. In some spreads, which have front support wings lower than the side back supports, a dog approaching at an acute angle may mistake the side of the front support for the jump and earn a refusal by clearing the wrong part of the jump.

Tires demand that the dog jump longer than normal for several reasons. First, the tire is much narrower than any other jump so the dog has to be technically more accurate to get through cleanly. With an average depth of 4", the tire acts like a mini-spread jump. The tire also has a "ceiling" that forces the dog to regulate the height of his jump.

Panel jumps present problems, especially for fast dogs. The panel is considered a *blind jump* because the dog can't see what is on the other side until he gets over the jump. This restriction makes it more difficult for a dog to gather himself for a subsequent obstacle like a contact or weaves.

2

Challenges

Known as handling challenges by judges and "traps" by handlers, a variety of obstacle configurations can cause handlers special concern. Listed here are the most common types of challenges: obstacle discriminations, options, handler restrictions, directional discriminations, and approach and spacing problems.

Obstacle Discriminations

Two obstacles of different characteristics placed in close proximity present the handler with an obstacle discrimination problem, the most common of the discrimination problems. The most common obstacle discrimination is a tunnel placed next to or under a contact with both the ramp of the contact and the tunnel opening facing the dog, as in **Figure 2-1**. Examples of other common obstacle discrimination problems are shown in **Figure 2-2**.

Figure 2-1. In a typical tunnel/ contact discrimination problem, the lead-in jump faces the dog toward both the up ramp of the A-frame and the tunnel entrance.

Figure 2-2. Other typical obstacle discrimination problems tantalize the dog with roughly equal access to two obstacles in close proximity and challenge the handler to guide his dog to the correct one.

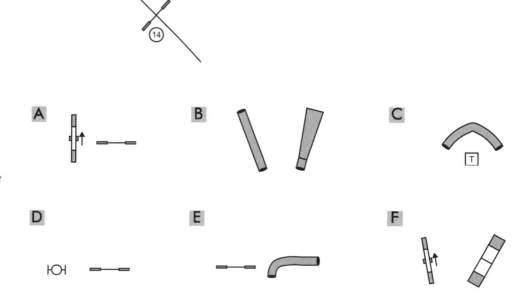

In obstacle discriminations, several factors can increase or decrease the difficulty of the problem. **Figure 2-3** illustrates how difficult approach angles to the correct obstacle, increased speed, or short spacing to the discrimination problem all increase the challenge of directing the dog to the correct obstacle. Conversely, **Figure 2-4** shows how softer angles, slower speed, or increased spacing between the preceding obstacle and the discrimination problem all help reduce the challenge. In addition, the distance between the two obstacles, the similarity of the two discrimination obstacles, and the dominance of one obstacle over the other (in the dog's and/or the handler's mind) all factor into assessing the difficulty of an obstacle discrimination problem. The closer the two obstacles are to each other, the more alike they are, or the more dominant one obstacle appears than the other—all serve to increase the difficulty of the challenge, as illustrated in **Figure 2-5**.

Figure 2-3. If the A-frame is the intended obstacle after the jump, all three lead-in sequences <u>increase</u> the difficulty of the discrimination problem. In A, a difficult approach angle to the A-frame increases the chance of the dog going into the tunnel. In B, the dog's greater speed generated over two jumps before the challenge increases his chance of going directly into tunnel. In C, the short distance between the jump and the A-frame requires a quicker response from the dog and handler to avoid the tunnel.

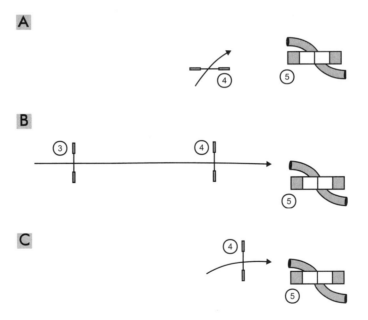

Judges classify obstacle discrimination problems as *major* and *minor*, depending on the proximity of the two obstacles to each other. In this book, we will consider discrimination problems in a broad sense. For a more complete discussion of discrimination problems, please refer to the first book in the series, *Fundamentals of Course Design for Dog Agility*.

Figure 2-4. If the A-frame is the intended obstacle after the jump, all three lead-in sequences lessen the difficulty of the discrimination problem. In A, a softer angle of approach makes it easier to get the dog to the A-frame. In B, after stopping on the table, the dog will have less chance to build up speed going into the problem, making it easier to direct him to the correct obstacle. In C, the increased distance between the jump and A-frame allows the handler more time to redirect the dog to the correct obstacle.

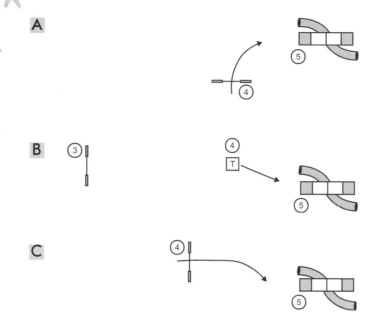

Figure 2-5. Assuming that the pipe tunnel is the off-course obstacle, all three examples on the left are considered harder to perform correctly than the ones on the right. In A, the spacing between the tunnel opening and the A-frame ramp makes the discrimination on the left more difficult than the one on the right. In B, the similarity between the pipe tunnel and collapsed tunnel makes the discrimination on the left more difficult than the one with the pipe tunnel and jump. In C, the tunnel is a much more dominant obstacle than the table.

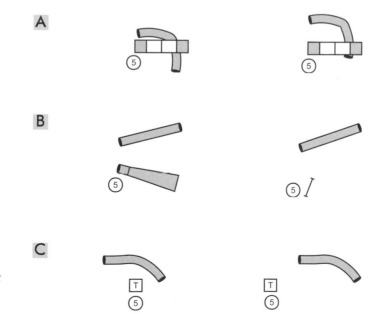

Options

Option problems are a specialized form of obstacle discrimination in which the obstacles that make up the discrimination are of the same type or nearly so. Thus, the handler cannot give a verbal cue as easily to tell the dog which obstacle to take. In the typical option problem presented in **Figure 2-6**, the logical path from jump #4 leads to the right opening of the curved pipe tunnel, but the left opening is the correct entrance. The handler can't give the dog a *Tunnel* command since it could signal the dog to go in either end. The handler can't even use a *Left* or *Come* command since both tunnel openings beckon to the dog's left. Clearly the handler needs to do something more to direct his dog successfully. **Figure 2-7** shows examples of common option problems.

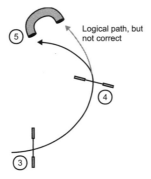

Figure 2-6. An option problem is a specialized type of obstacle discrimination problem in which the handler must direct his dog to discriminate correctly between two obstacles of the same type or, in this case, two openings of the same tunnel.

Figure 2-7. Typical option problems like these present the handler with the special challenge of finding a means other than verbal obstacle commands to cue his dog to the correct obstacle.

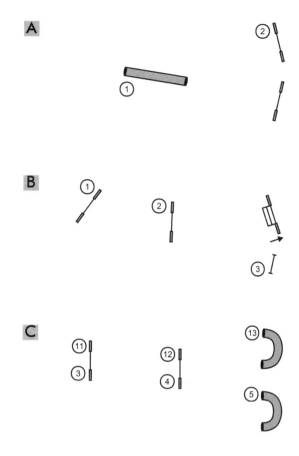

Handler Restrictions

A handler restriction problem arises when an obstacle or object impedes or blocks the typical path of a handler. A handler restriction challenges the handler to direct his dog at an increased distance or to operate on the other side of his dog than he would normally. Two types of handler restrictions exist. An *absolute* restriction, illustrated in **Figure 2-8,** forces the handler to operate on the opposite of the typical or expected side. It's called absolute because the handler has no options at all. In this case, since the wall of the ring is right next to the #9 jump, the handler can't send the dog over that jump on his left, yet he must change the dog's path from the #8 to the #9 jump. This setup forces the handler to switch sides. A handler who can only run his dog on the heel side will run into trouble in this sequence since he will likely have to cross somewhere to put the dog on the right for jump #9. Fortunately, these types of problems are rarely seen these days.

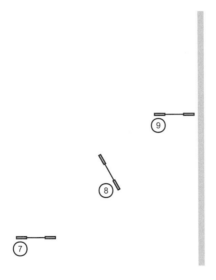

Figure 2-8. With winged jump #9 positioned right at the ring boundary, the handler has no option but to handle the dog on his right. Absolute handler restrictions such as this force the handler to work on the side opposite the one he would normally choose.

The second and more popular type of handler restriction is the *elective* restriction problem, so named because the handler has the choice to work on one side or the other to handle the challenge. However, an elective restriction problem is designed so that there is a distinct advantage in being on one side as opposed to the other. In **Figure 2-9,** for example, the heel-side handler can still perform this sequence, but the tunnel potentially will push him further away from the dog on the descent contact than he would like. In addition, the heel-side handler may have a harder time turning his dog to the #6 jump. A handler who can cross somewhere before or after the A-frame will be at an advantage over one who cannot. **Figure 2-10** shows some common elective restriction challenges.

Figure 2-9. An elective handler restriction allows the handler to work on either side of his dog but offers an advantage in working on one side over the other. In this example, working the dog on the left is possible, but it will force the handler to be farther away from his dog on the contact than if he handled the sequence with the dog on the right.

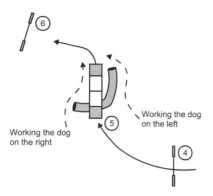

Figure 2-10. In all three examples of elective handler restrictions here, the handler can gain an advantage by layering obstacles, placing an obstacle between him and his dog.

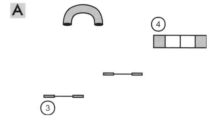

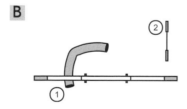

A useful handling maneuver to mention in dealing with elective restrictions is the concept of *layering*. A handler is said to be layering an obstacle when he puts an obstacle between him and his dog, temporarily increasing the distance between them. The advantage of layering is that the handler can avoid entering a tight portion of the course where his presence might force his dog onto the wrong obstacle. In **Figure 2-11A**, for example, a handler who runs past #3 and the unmarked jump risks pushing the dog into the tunnel instead of turning the dog to the A-frame. This is especially true if the dog is ahead of the handler. The handler who goes into "the pocket," as in **Figure 2-11B**, will have to slow the dog substantially if he is going to keep him out of the tunnel and will have to work harder at getting his dog's attention to turn him to the A-frame. A handler who can layer the unmarked jump, as in **Figure 2-11c**, should have an easier time turning the dog to the A-frame without undue loss of speed.

Figure 2-11. In A, the handler runs past #3, courting disaster with an off-course into the tunnel. In B, the handler goes into the pocket, creating a time-wasting, loopy approach to the A-frame as he tries to avoid the tunnel. In C, the handler layers the unmarked jump and works his dog at a distance, gaining a faster, surer approach to the A-frame.

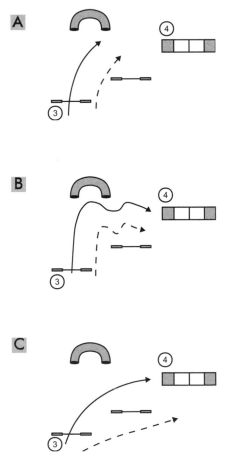

Directional Discriminations

Directional discriminations challenge a dog to choose a direction: typically right or left, get out or come in, or turn or go straight. In most cases, an obstacle configuration called a *box formation* or a *jump box*, as illustrated in **Figure 2-12**, presents directional discriminations. In this case, the dog entering the box can opt to go right, left, or straight. Often as not, because of the earlier handling requirements of the course, the handler will be on the opposite side of the intended turn direction. To negotiate the sequence successfully requires the handler to give a directional cue, either verbal or visual, to aim the dog in the correct direction. These challenges can be some of the more difficult course problems to solve, especially with a fast dog that is way out in front of his handler.

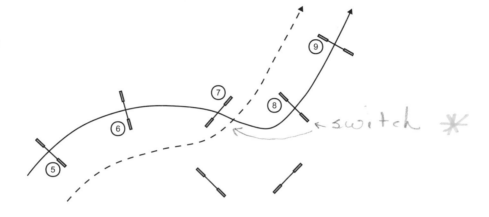

Figure 2-12. This typical directional discrimination problem challenges the handler to guide his dog correctly through the box of jumps and execute a change of sides.

Spacing Problems

The distances and angles between jumps in a sequence can present profound handling challenges. In lower level classes, the jumps tend to be evenly and widely spaced. As the class level increases, so does the difficulty of spatial challenges. In the upper division levels, such as USDAA Masters or AKC Excellent, the distance between obstacles can vary rapidly and drastically from absolute minimums to absolute maximums. Variable spacing problems, as shown in **Figure 2-13**, challenge the handler to get his dog to either shorten or lengthen stride to accommodate the changes in distance. Failure to adjust commonly results in displaced bars. In addition, the jump angles as well as the stagger of the jumps, that is, the degree to which the jumps are offset from a straight line, can vary extensively over a short distance, as illustrated in **Figure 2-14**. Each problem offers a different handling challenge. In either case, the most common course faults are refusal penalties or knocked bars. Frequently, a particularly difficult jump sequence, as in **Figure 2-15**, combines all three types of spacing problems.

Figure 2-13. A shows typical even, generous spacing of obstacles on a novice course. B shows the irregular obstacle spacing typical of upper level sequences.

Figure 2-14. The A sequence shows angled jumping; the B sequence shows a staggered line of jumps.

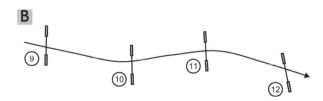

Figure 2-15. Upper level courses, such as USDAA Masters and AKC Excellent, typically combine problems of variable distance, angulation, and stagger to create difficult jumping sequences like this one.

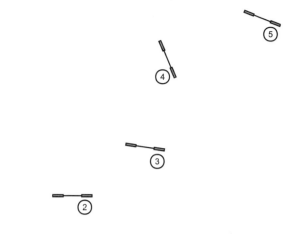

Approaches

While not high on the average handler's list of challenges, the way a dog approaches an obstacle can create major problems. For example, the approach to the weaves as shown in **Figure 2-16** is straightforward enough that the average dog should be able to make this entrance easily. In **Figure 2-17**, however, the #4 jump has been moved 6' closer to the poles, about 5' to the right, and rotated. Now the dog has to turn much harder to get into the weaves. Moreover, the increased distance between the jumps #3 and #4 will make the dog land longer from #4, causing more of an overrun. The handler will have to work much harder to make the weave pole entrance and keep the dog from getting a refusal or runout. Considering the dog's approach to an obstacle is especially important for the weave poles and contacts because the performance criteria for these obstacles are tougher than those for jumps and tunnels.

Figure 2-16. A gentle arc of jumps that aims the dog directly to the correct weave pole entry makes this an easy approach.

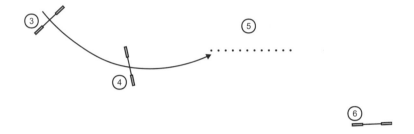

Figure 2-17. Contrast this more challenging approach to the weave poles with that in Figure 2-16. The handler will have to work hard here to get the weave pole entry and avoid a refusal or a runout.

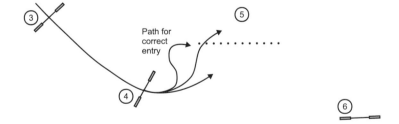

3 Handling Maneuvers

The term *handling maneuver* describes any movement that the handler uses to influence the way a dog moves through a course. A handling maneuver can be as simple as moving forward in a straight line to get the dog to move forward straight ahead or a much more complex movement that requires a more thorough explanation of what it is and why and when to use it.

It's critical to keep in mind that handlers are constantly giving their dogs signals—intentional or not. Dogs are astonishingly perceptive at picking up on these cues and responding to them. See "A Hierarchy of Cues" (page 46) for more on how handlers can use cues effectively to control a dog's path.

Before discussing handling maneuvers, I need to explain a couple of terms. The first is *handler focus*, which describes the dog's focus on the handler to the exclusion of the obstacles. Handler focus is what gives us control to move the dog away from obstacles, to turn him when we turn, and to slow him when we slow. A handler-focused dog generally looks more for his handler, turns more toward his handler, works closer to the handler, and takes obstacles only when his handler says to. This type of focus is important on tight courses with sharp turns, courses that present discrimination challenges, and Snooker courses. Most handler maneuvers put the dog into handler focus to some extent because dogs are so sensitive to our body language, especially to our movement. Generally, a dog keys on the motion first and on body language second. That is why when a handler turns his body quickly but continues to run forward, the dog typically continues straight ahead instead of turning.

The opposite of handler focus is *obstacle focus*, which means that the dog is more focused on the obstacles than on his handler. Obstacle focus gives the dog his speed, allows the handler to work at a distance, and motivates the dog to move toward obstacles even if the handler is heading in a different direction. An obstacle–focused dog looks for the handler less, is more apt to take obstacles on his own, tends to be faster on course, and tends to work at a distance more easily. This type of focus is important in wide-open courses with lots of space between obstacles, sweeping turns, handler restriction problems, or games such as Gamblers that require independent distance work from the dog. Most directional cues rely on obstacle focus for their successful execution.

A dog rarely tends to be solely handler-focused or solely obstacle-focused. Generally, the dog's focus is a blend of the two, although the dog will tend to default more toward one type of focus than the other. The art is in determining which focus the dog tends toward and how to channel that focus. To run agility courses well, the handler must learn how to switch his dog back and forth between handler and obstacle focus as the situation demands.

Rear Cross

Also known as a *back cross* or a *cross behind*, this maneuver turns a dog away from the handler as the handler changes sides to his dog. With the dog ahead of him, the handler crosses behind the dog to turn him in the new direction. There are two types of rear crosses. In the *soft rear cross*, as in **Figure 3-1**, the handler gradually changes from one side to the other, generally starting the cross closer to the obstacle preceding the direction change. Because the dog gets more notice that he needs to change leads (See "The Concept of Leads," page 53), this strategy allows a more efficient turn and minimizes spins (also called *donuts*), wide turns, and dropped bars. In a *dramatic* rear cross, illustrated in **Figure 3-2**, the handler changes direction much closer to the obstacle that he needs to cross behind. Although some handlers believe that a quick, pronounced change of direction can turn a dog faster, most feel that a dramatic rear cross makes the dog turn wider or turn in the wrong direction because the dog gets virtually no warning about the direction change.

Figure 3-1. In a soft rear cross, the handler gradually changes sides from left to right, giving his dog plenty of time—and notice—to change direction. The handler starts the cross at the obstacle preceding the direction change, in this case, jump #6.

Figure 3-2. In a dramatic rear cross, the handler abruptly crosses behind his dog, giving him little or no warning of the change of direction. The cross is executed close to the obstacle that the handler needs to cross behind, jump #7 in this case. Spins, wide turns, and displaced bars are the common result.

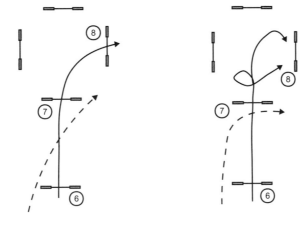

Crossing behind the dog may look simple, but it poses risks. To execute a rear cross successfully, a handler has to have his dog out in front of him. Being even with or ahead of the dog won't do, since the handler will have to slow down to allow the dog to catch up before he can execute the rear cross. The handler's slowing down will make the dog slow down, so the handler won't be able to cross behind his dog at all. In addition, performing a rear cross is difficult for a slow dog that runs behind or at the side of his handler since the handler can't communicate the direction change until very late. Therefore, for slow dogs, the rear cross tends to slow them down even more.

When attempting a rear cross, handlers frequently end up pushing the dog off the jump, causing a handler-induced refusal. In addition, a poorly executed rear cross often causes the dog to spin in the wrong direction, turn wide, or drop a jump bar.

Front Cross

With a front cross—the opposite of a rear cross—the handler attempts to influence the dog's movement and direction by moving or crossing in front of the dog, as illustrated in **Figure 3-3**. In a front cross, a handler typically crosses the dog's path as the dog is approaching or in the process of taking an obstacle. Since the handler is in front of the dog, a front cross allows the dog to more easily pick up the direction change and alter leads to accommodate the new direction or side change. In a front cross, the handler gets in front of the dog and, never taking his eyes off the dog, reverses his direction by turning toward the dog. Once completed, the dog should be on the opposite side of the handler from where he started.

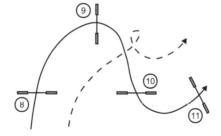

Figure 3-3. So-named because the handler gets in front of his dog, a well-executed front cross gives the dog ample warning of the impending change of direction (and lead).

A properly executed front cross can tighten a turn for several reasons. First, because the handler acts as the focus and anchor or pivot point for the turn, the dog can turn tighter. Second, since the front cross focuses the dog on his handler, the dog isn't looking for the next obstacle and thus slows down, which always allows him to make a tighter turn. Finally, with the handler being in front of the dog, he can give the dog directional information much earlier so that the dog can turn more than with a rear cross. Front crosses are especially efficient with slower dogs and in situations demanding a tight turn to the next obstacle.

One misconception about the front cross is that it tends to speed up slower dogs. For slower dogs that run next to or trail behind the handler, the dog's speed usually depends on the handler's motion. In reality, the front cross doesn't speed up the dog; it just doesn't let the dog's speed bleed off since the handler is moving a great deal more with a front cross than he does with a rear cross.

For a handler to execute an efficient front cross, he must be out ahead of the dog enough so that, as he slows down to start the cross, the dog can pick up the visual signal, gear down, and execute a tight turn. While getting out in front of the dog sounds easy, it isn't always. If a handler rushes to try to get ahead of his dog to cross in front, often the dog will try to catch up with him, accelerating just as the handler starts the cross. Caught off guard by the sudden change of direction, the dog slides around the turn in a wide arc and the nonplussed handler stops, which slows the dog down. Frequently, the result is a wider, slower turn than it would have been with a rear cross.

A variation of the front cross, known as the *twizzle* or *Axford axel*, is named for Alaina Axford-Moore of Pennsylvania, the first handler to use it regularly. The maneuver resembles a front cross except that the handler only changes sides, not direction. This maneuver is useful if you want to keep an essentially straight line, but need to change sides to help set a sequence, as in **Figure 3-4.**

Figure 3-4. The Twizzle or Axford Axel is a front cross in which the handler simply changes sides, not direction, for easier handling. Here the handler needs to perform the weave poles with the dog on the left, but will have an easier time if the dog is on his right side for #2 through #4.

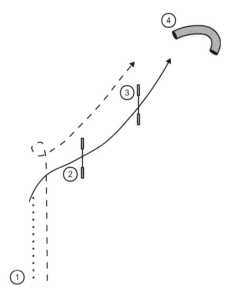

Blind Cross

Most of the requirements for the front cross also apply to the blind cross. The handler needs to be ahead of his dog. The difference between a front cross and a blind cross is that instead of turning toward his dog, as in **Figure 3-5A**, the handler turns away from the dog and changes sides with his back to the dog, as in **Figure 3-5B**. For a second, then, the dog is out of sight. Once the cross is completed, the dog ends up on the opposite side of the handler.

Figure 3-5. In A, the handler executes a front cross, turning into his dog and then heading in the new direction. In the blind cross shown in B, the handler is also ahead of his dog. However, with the blind cross, the handler turns away from his dog and then picks him up on the opposite side, heading in the new direction. Of necessity, the handler loses sight of his dog for a second.

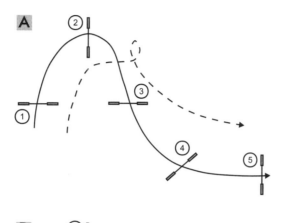

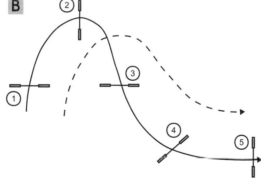

A properly executed blind cross is faster than a front cross for several reasons. First, the handler isn't stopping, reversing direction, or staring down the dog, so the handler can move faster in the new direction than with a front cross, which speeds up his dog. Second, since the handler doesn't remain in front of his dog as much or as long as in a front cross, a blind cross minimizes the dog's handler focus, so a blind cross promotes a dog's switching faster from handler focus to obstacle focus. The dog picks up the next obstacle and speeds toward it faster. Third, the blind cross can give a lead-out advantage to the handler since he doesn't spend as much time executing the cross.

The blind cross presents a couple of disadvantages, as well. A blind cross requires that the handler lose sight of—and break contact with—his dog for a second. A handler who is slow in turning thus runs the risk of losing track of which side his dog is on. Frequently, a poorly executed blind cross will result in a wide turn with the dog on the wrong side of the handler. The other problem is that the speed that the blind cross generates can cause the dog to jump long in the turn and thus increase the challenge of making a sharp turn after the cross. Thus, blind crosses are best used in sequences where the handler needs to change sides and keep up speed but doesn't need to make a rapid, sharp turn immediately after he completes the cross.

Counter Rotation

Also known as a *tandem turn*, the counter-rotation, or *CR*, is identical in requirements, advantages, and disadvantages to the front cross. The difference is that in a front cross, the dog is in the beginning or middle of performing an obstacle as the handler executes the cross. In a CR, however, the dog has completed, or has almost completed, the preceding obstacle when the handler executes the cross, as shown in **Figure 3-6**. Thus, the CR is more of a landing-side turn and change of sides, whereas the front cross is more of a takeoff-side turn and change of sides. Moreover, in a CR, the dog turns directly toward the handler, while in a front cross, the dog moves in an arc around the handler. A CR is best used when the course requires a side change coupled with a quick 180° turn back over the original path.

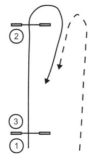

Figure 3-6. Similar to a front cross, a counter-rotation (CR) or tandem turn accomplishes a change of sides and of direction when the handler turns toward his dog. It's chiefly used as a landing-side cue as opposed to the front cross, which is primarily a takeoff-side cue.

Reverse Flow Pivot

This maneuver, attributed to Jim Basic from California, was used to describe how Jim's fast dog could switch directions rapidly and come in close to his handler without Jim apparently breaking stride or screaming at the dog to *Come!* At a seminar, Marquand Cheek, another Californian, jokingly offered the term *reverse flow pivot* or *RFP*, and the name stuck.

In an RFP, shown in **Figure 3-7**, the start of the maneuver resembles the front cross and the CR; the difference lies in the finish. In the front cross and CR, the handler turns into the dog and changes sides. In the RFP, the handler turns into the dog and then immediately pivots away from the dog, keeping the dog on the same side as when he started. In response to the handler's initial turn, the dog turns and comes in toward the handler. Pivoting in place, the handler then reverses direction, turning away from the dog. In response, the dog turns back to his original direction, but is now closer to the handler. So, the dog has tightened a turn and moved in closer to his handler, yet remains on the same side of the handler.

Figure 3-7. A reverse-flow pivot (RFP) requires a quick pivot toward and then away from the dog. This causes the dog to brake and pull in tighter to the handler. It's the agility equivalent of a head fake to adjust a dog's line without changing his direction.

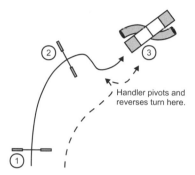

Handler pivots and reverses turn here.

The RFP is used to tighten a dog's turn significantly and quickly. It acts like a brake, allowing the handler to quickly slow and turn the dog. It can be used in a sequence similar to that illustrated in Figure 3-7, where the expected path of the dog takes him to the wrong obstacle. While effective, an RFP should only be used occasionally. Because the maneuver is a "head fake" that makes a dog turn first one way and then the other in rapid order, it should not be used as a routine way of turning most dogs. For a dog lacking high drive, overusing the RFP may slow the dog when it's not necessary, since he is constantly guessing when he will need to turn tight.

V-Set

A V-set is any maneuver in which the handler sets up the dog to turn in the correct direction before the dog actually needs to turn. The V-set enables the handler to avoid off-courses and call-offs by aiming the dog in the new direction well in advance and by removing off-course obstacles from the dog's line of vision. The handler is generally on the inside of the turn, and the dog is on the outside, away from the obstacle at the onset of the turn.

In **Figure 3-8A**, the dog's expected path is to the A-frame, but he needs to turn to the teeter. One handling maneuver is to try a front cross between jump #8 and the A-frame to turn the dog to the teeter. However, if the handler can't get there in time, he will push the dog up the A-frame. In addition, the A-frame will be the closest large obstacle to the handler when he executes the cross. Another possible maneuver is to start with the dog on the right and to cross behind jump #8 to turn the dog, as in **Figure 3-8B**. However, if the dog fails to pick up on the cross, or is even late in picking up the cross, he'll head right up the A-frame or have a loopy path to the teeter. The handler can scream and yell, *No! Come!* We all know how well that works most of the time.

Figure 3-8. In A, the handler is likely to have difficulty getting to the front cross position, so he may push the dog up the A-frame. In B, a rear cross will amount to a last-minute attempt to pull the dog away from the off-course A-frame at jump #8 and will typically fail completely or result in a run-out or a loopy approach to the teeter.

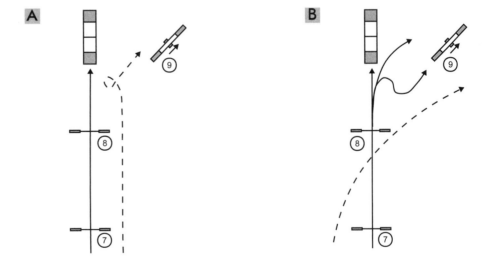

Instead, if the handler were able to push his dog slightly to the left between the two jumps and then turn to the right, as in **Figure 3-9A**, the dog would be heading directly toward the teeter. Executing a V-set takes the A-frame out of the dog's vision and puts the teeter in view instead, making it much easier to get the dog to take the teeter. In essence, the V-set can be considered a takeoff-side turn, providing the dog with information *before* the jump about where he needs to move and what obstacle he needs to take, rather than *after* the jump, as is the case in Figure 3-8A and 3-8B. Usually the V-set turn is faster for several reasons. First, the dog focuses on the correct obstacle rather than the wrong obstacle. Second, the dog doesn't have to keep looking at the handler for direction. Third, in comparing the paths in **Figure 3-9B**, the V-set path, while slightly longer between the two jumps, is actually shorter overall. All these factors make for a faster, cleaner turn to the teeter. V-sets can prove invaluable in dealing with obstacle or directional discriminations, option problems, or approach problems.

Figure 3-9. In a V-set, the handler pushes the dog into the V-point. A properly executed V-set, like the one in A, not only aims the dog at the intended obstacle (the teeter) but also takes the dominant off-course obstacle (the A-frame) out of the dog's view. B shows that the V-set path, while slightly longer between the two jumps, is shorter overall.

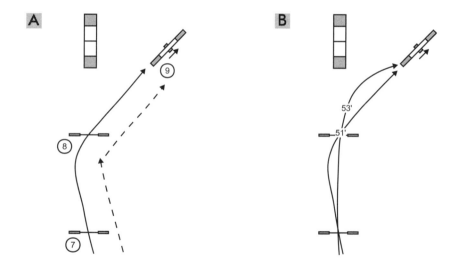

If the handler is on the outside of an intended change of direction, as in **Figure 3–10**, he can perform the *reverse*, or *counter V-set (counter V)*. Rules and principles for V-sets also apply to the counter V-set. To execute a counter V, the handler 1) pulls, instead of pushing, the dog to the V-point; 2) pushes the dog toward the intended obstacle; and 3) crosses behind him. The result is a V-set turn and a change of sides. The first drawback of the reverse V is that the dog stays focused on the handler while he is setting the V. For a dog that already is too handler-focused, turning him away from his handler to take the intended obstacle can cause a displaced bar or a refusal. The second drawback is that if a dog loses handler focus when the handler moves away from the intended obstacle, he may take the obstacle at the wrong angle, leaving the handler moving in the wrong direction on the wrong side of the turn, as in **Figure 3–11**. This is why many experienced handlers think of the reverse V-set as one of the more complex handling maneuvers to master.

Figure 3-10. In a reverse V-set, the handler 1) pulls the dog into the V-point; 2) pushes the dog toward the correct obstacle; and 3) crosses behind the dog. The reverse V-set is a useful maneuver when the handler is on the outside of an upcoming change of direction.

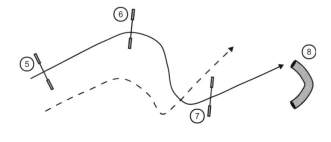

Figure 3-11. A failed reverse V-set like this one, where the dog lost focus on the handler's cues, leaves the handler on the wrong side of the turn, headed in the wrong direction.

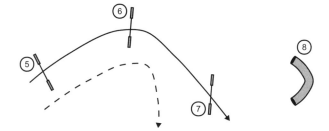

Lead-Out Advantage

Provided one has a dog that can wait at the start line, the lead-out is one of the easiest—but also one of the most misunderstood and misapplied—handler maneuvers. Most handlers think of a lead-out advantage as putting a dog on a stay at the start line, going out a distance, and calling the dog over the first obstacle(s), as illustrated in **Figure 3-12**. The dual purpose of this lead-out is to give the slower handler with a faster dog a head start and to enable a handler to get into position to turn his dog.

Figure 3-12. A lead-out at the start line, in which the handler gets a head start on his dog by one or more obstacles, gives the handler more time to set up his dog for turns, obstacle discriminations, and the like.

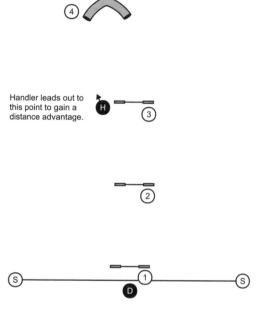

Handler leads out to this point to gain a distance advantage.

This is all well and good, but what many handlers forget is that to gain from the advantage they purportedly have given themselves, they need to move and communicate with the dog that is rapidly catching up to them. Many a flat-footed handler finds that his dog runs by him, starts heading in the wrong direction, and has to be called off an obstacle. Frequently the result is a wrong course despite the call-off, a wide turn, a displaced bar, or a demotivated dog. Often a shorter lead-out is better if it gets the handler to move a little sooner and cues the dog earlier about what is going to happen next.

While handlers typically employ lead-outs at the start line, they can use them to their advantage any time they can get significantly in front of the dog. One obvious place is a table, as in **Figure 3-13,** where the dog is temporarily motionless. **Figure 3-14** shows a different example in which the handler sends his dog in one direction (to the tunnel) while he moves in the opposite direction. While the dog runs the longer route, the handler "cheats" and cuts the corner to get a head start on setting up the dog for the obstacle discrimination sequence.

Figure 3-13. On-course lead-outs are possible whenever the dog is stationary, typically when he is on the table, or when the handler can get significantly ahead of his dog.

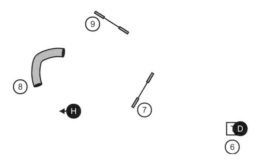

Figure 3-14. In this on-course lead-out, the handler sends his dog to the tunnel while he moves in the other direction. This maneuver puts the handler in a better position to manage the A-frame/tunnel discrimination than if he were to run the entire sequence with his dog.

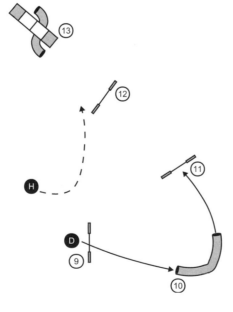

One variation of the lead-out is known as the *lead-out pivot*. It starts as a lead-out but instead of moving off in the direction he is facing, the handler pivots 270° into the dog to turn him at a right angle to his original path, as in **Figure 3-15**. Like a stationary front cross, this maneuver turns the dog more quickly. If the dog is caught by surprise, however, he either can go wide (since the handler originally was in a lead-out position facing forward) or he can drop a bar if he's not ready for the pivot and turns too quickly.

Figure 3-15. In a lead-out pivot, the handler leads out facing forward, then pivots 270° into his dog to turn him 90° over the #3 jump. The maneuver resembles a stationary front cross.

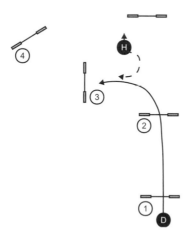

A Heirarchy of Cues

One of the things an agility instructor usually tells a new student is that dogs respond to body cues, such as which way the handler is facing or which way he turns his shoulders. As the student advances in training and begins running sequences, he sees these concepts demonstrated. Often when a dog begins getting ahead of his handler, the dog doesn't respond as quickly or as accurately as when he was behind or even with the handler. Sometimes the dog fails to respond at all.

What causes this lack of response? Why is it that the dog turns when the handler is closer but doesn't when the handler is behind? Is the dog purposely ignoring the handler's body cues?

To understand this problem from the dog's perspective, we need to consider how a dog sees. Above all, dogs are primed to see motion and detect even the slightest twitch in other animals—and in their handlers.

A dog views objects in one of two ways: with *central vision* or *peripheral vision*. When a dog uses his central vision, he's looking at what's right in front of him, directly in his line of sight. When a dog is behind or even with his handler, he can see the way the handler is facing, how the handler moves or turns his body, arms, or feet, and whether the handler shifts his position. If a dog could count and talk, he could probably even tell you how many fingers the handler was holding up. In other words, a dog picks up on many cues about how to move from the handler, and to the dog, the detail of these cues is quite clear.

If the dog continues to face forward but the handler starts drifting to the side or behind him, the dog will start using peripheral vision. In peripheral vision, cues are much blurrier, and details that the dog previously picked up on are not as clear. Sometimes the dog cannot determine which way a handler is facing or turning.

The dog, however, can see, and will respond to motion—that is, whether the handler is moving forward or moving backward. When the handler is only slightly behind or to the side of the dog, the dog can see *lateral movement* (sideways movement). As the handler continues to drop behind the dog, the dog begins to lose the ability to distinguish detail in motion so that, even if a handler runs forward and to the right, often the dog will only move forward.

What does our understanding of the dog's perception have to do with control of a dog on an agility course? Let's take a dog that is running beside the handler over two jumps, set at right angles to each other. As the handler approaches the first jump and the dog jumps it, the handler, maintaining constant speed, turns in the new direction. Most likely, the dog will turn in the new direction, see the next jump, and take it.

In the same sequence, if the dog is slightly ahead of his handler when the handler turns to the next jump, the dog will probably lag slightly in his turn since he can't see the turn cue as clearly. The dog will still turn but the turn may be slightly wider or slower. If the dog is still further out in front of the handler and the handler tries to turn the dog as before, the dog often fails to turn, turns extremely wide, and/or may miss the jump entirely.

What happened? As the handler got further behind the dog, the dog lost the ability to see the turn cues as accurately or as quickly. Details about the turn were lost or blurred as the handler disappeared behind the dog. Remember, the handler was moving at a constant speed so that his motion told the dog to move forward. When the handler turned, the dog couldn't easily pick up the direction in which the handler was facing. Thus, the dog didn't turn as quickly or as tightly.

What can the handler do to help the dog if the dog is working ahead of him? The typical solution is for the handler to hang back from the second jump, stop suddenly, and yell, *Come!* Another common solution is for the handler to turn his shoulders in the new direction sooner and more quickly, to give the dog a more visible and timely cue to the upcoming change of direction. In both cases, the dog typically still turns wide and more slowly to the next jump. Often the dog turns as if the handler hadn't stopped or called him at all. What else could the handler do? Instead of stopping suddenly when approaching the first jump, the handler should start slowing slightly. His deceleration should put the dog on alert so that the dog will start slowing as well, which will shorten the dog's stride slightly. Only then should the handler begin to turn in the new direction. The dog's resulting turn should be much tighter and slightly faster.

For comparison's sake, imagine a driver going 70 mph on a straight line and approaching a turn designed for 40 mph. If the driver waited until he got to the turn, then tried to hit the brakes hard and turn, the car might make the turn but would most likely side-slip or skid wide and slow. In addition, the driver would have to hold on hard to make the turn. If this same driver knew that the turn were coming up, he could ease off the accelerator and apply the brakes softly, allowing a slower approach than in the first example. The resulting turn would be tighter and faster since not so much of the car's momentum would be going into skidding or side-slipping. In addition, the driver would need to put less energy into holding the turn.

Changes in motion are the most powerful way to control a dog's path because the dog tends to pick up this type of cue over a wider range of handler positions. Regardless of whether the dog is in front, beside, or behind the handler, dogs sense motion and, more importantly, changes in motion.

Because dogs generally tend to cue on motion more readily than any other handler cues, regardless of the position of the handler, we can say that motion sits at the top of a hierarchy of control cues. When a dog has the handler in central or in slight peripheral vision, the dog tends to cue first on the handler's motion and next on the handler's body position—which arm he is extending or which way he is facing. Sometimes, when the dog is on central focus, the handler's body position can be as dominant a cue as the handler's motion. Dogs tend to cue on a verbal command last, and then only when the handler disappears from peripheral vision entirely. Once the handler disappears from the dog's peripheral vision, the handler only has verbal cues to steer the dog. Those handlers that are constantly far behind their dogs tend to rely more on verbal cues to control their dogs since the dogs have no detectable motion or body cues to guide them.

As long as the control cues agree with one another, everything is fine for the dog. If a dog is on the handler's right side, for instance, and the handler extends his right arm to the right, tells the dog to turn right, and moves to the right, he will likely get the dog to turn right. Conversely, if the handler extends his right arm to the right, tells the dog to turn right, but then moves left, the dog will often follow the handler's body cue and turn to the left. When cues are in conflict, the dog resorts to the control hierarchy and responds to the most dominant cue, that is, the one closest to the top of the hierarchy. Since motion is more dominant than body position cues or verbal cues, the dog initially goes with the motion cue.

The more the handler gives conflicting cues, the more confused the dog gets. Thus, when running an agility sequence, it is important to keep the cues in harmony with one another and to know which cue would be more effective, based on the relative position of the handler to the dog.

4   Directional Cues

Almost anything that a handler does or says can be construed as a *directional cue*. A handler who turns to the right communicates to the dog to turn right, even if the handler doesn't say anything. Although any handler maneuver can be considered a directional cue, for this section we will focus on verbal cues.

While most handlers think of verbal directional cues as simply *Left* and *Right*, directional cues encompass many more options, such as *Back*, *Away*, *Turn*, or *This Way*. In fact, a handler can use any word or phrase to denote a direction change that he can come up with (if it makes sense to the dog and more important, if the handler can remember it). It is critical that the word or phrase be short enough so that the handler doesn't take too long saying it. This type of verbal cue is largely self-explanatory and need not be covered here. What remains are two vital commands: *Go On* and *Get Out*.

Go On

Go On, or simply *Go*, tells the dog to continue in the direction he is moving even if his handler starts dropping behind. This command has practical applications in agility where the handler is much slower than the dog. Instead of having the dog slow to keep pace with the handler, the handler can command *Go* to get the dog moving ahead in a sequence and prevent the dog from slowing down. The *Go* command can also prevent the dog from turning prematurely toward an unwanted obstacle if the handler gets too far behind.

Get Out

Arguably the more important of the two directional commands discussed here, *Get Out*, or simply *Out*, tells the dog that his handler is going to parallel his direction but that the lateral distance between them will increase. *Get Out* is not only a vital command for Gamblers but is also useful on courses that present handler restrictions or that offer the handler the opportunity to layer an obstacle. Although most take this command to mean that the dog needs to move away from the handler, it can also mean that the handler can move away from the dog.

In **Figure 4-1**, as the handler runs with the dog to the tunnel, the distance between them remains relatively constant. In **Figure 4-2**, the handler stays on the same path as in Figure 4-1, but commands the dog to *Get Out*, signaling the dog to push away from the handler and take the straight tunnel. This maneuver is known as a Type I *Get Out*. In **Figure 4-3**, the handler directs his dog to *Get Out* but then shifts his own path to the right. In effect, the *Get Out* command here signals the dog to keep the original line to the curved tunnel while his handler moves away from him. This is known as a Type II *Get Out*. In both cases, the lateral distance increases: In the first case, the handler pushes the dog away from him, and in the second, the handler pushes away from the dog. The path the handler takes immediately after he gives the *Get Out* cue determines which type of *Get Out* the handler has employed.

Figure 4-1. Here, the handler moves together and parallel with his dog to the curved tunnel. The distance between dog and handler remains relatively constant.

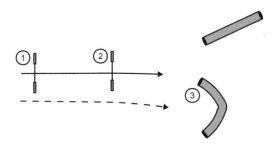

Figure 4-2. In a Type I Get Out, the handler pushes his dog away with the verbal command while he maintains his original line.

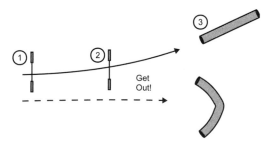

Figure 4-3. In the Type II Get Out, the dog continues on his original line while the handler gives the verbal command and moves away from the dog.

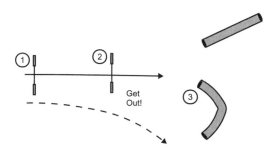

I have not mentioned the commands *Here* or *Come* as verbal directional cues even though handlers often use these cues to turn dogs. That is because for many dogs, these commands have become nonspecific. In other words, each of these commands has more than one meaning and hence can be confusing to the dog. If a handler commands *Come* but doesn't care how—or how fast—his dog gets back to him, the dog will learn that rocketing back to his handler, or hesitating, sniffing the ground, and then sauntering back to his handler both count as appropriate responses to the command *Come*. Another time the handler might use the command in a third meaning as an obedience *Come* and sit in front of the handler. In an agility context, *Come* can mean: take a jump, come away from an obstacle but keep moving in parallel to the handler, or come right to the handler avoiding any obstacles on the way. For our imaginary handler then, there are at least six different definitions of the command *Come*, and a bewildering assortment for the dog.

With other directional cues, such as *Right* or *Turn*, we can give more specific information. *Right* means turn right, regardless of which side the handler might be on. Furthermore, *Come* or *Here* are considered *landing-side* commands, directional cues issued once the dog is on the landing side of whatever obstacle he is performing. For instance, suppose a dog needs to perform two jumps at right angles to each other, as in **Figure 4-4**, and the handler is on the inside of the right turn. When does the handler command *Come* to turn his dog? Issued before the second jump of the turn, the command probably will pull the dog off the jump. Therefore the handler needs to tell the dog to *Come* on the landing side of the second jump. But the dog will land thinking he is going straight, so the *Come* command is late and leads to a wide turn. For this reason, either verbal or visual landing-side cues usually put the dog at a disadvantage on course. Thus, when walking a course, handlers should focus on a strategy that minimizes landing-side cues and optimizes takeoff-side cues.

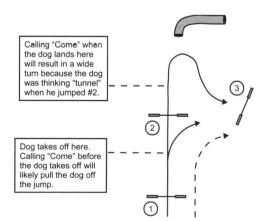

Figure 4-4. Calling "Come!" before jump #2 (a takeoff-side cue) may pull the dog off the jump. Calling "Come!" after jump #2 (a landing-side cue) usually results in a wide, loopy turn because the dog lands thinking he is going straight and gets the information too late to turn crisply to #3.

Calling "Come" when the dog lands here will result in a wide turn because the dog was thinking "tunnel" when he jumped #2.

Dog takes off here. Calling "Come" before the dog takes off will likely pull the dog off the jump.

5

The Concept of Leads

A handler can use directional cues and certain handler maneuvers to set up the dog

- For obstacle discrimination, handler-restriction, and option challenges

- For layering obstacles

- To turn the dog at a distance

- To take advantage of on-course lead-outs

More important, properly given directional cues are *takeoff* cues, issued on the takeoff side of an obstacle and hence early enough to allow the dog to plan his path before he lands. To understand why this timing is critical, we need to discuss the concept of leads.

Watch any four-legged animal canter in a straight line and you'll notice that the animal extends either the left foreleg or right foreleg out in front of the other foreleg when running. The favored front leg is generally known as the *lead leg* while the other foreleg is known as the *trail leg*. You'll see this phenomenon in any gait faster than a trot. An animal with the right leg in front is said to be on a *right lead* while an animal with the left leg in front is said to be on a *left lead*.

If a dog running on a right lead turns right, he maintains the right lead. If a dog running on a right lead turns left, with few exceptions, he switches leads to a left lead as he enters the turn. Known as *changing* or *shifting leads*, this switch is critical in understanding how a dog negotiates an agility course. What causes changes of lead?

Because the dog is four-legged, it requires some coordination of front and rear, left and right legs to remain in a balanced state. If a dog goes into a right turn on a right lead, his weight shifts to the inside so that he can make a balanced turn. If the dog goes into a left turn on a right lead, his weight shifts to the right and to the outside of the turn, placing him in an unbalanced state. Centrifugal force will push the dog's body away from the pivot point and make the turn wider. Known as a *counter-canter*, this type of off-lead turn not only is unbalanced, but uncomfortable as well. Anyone who has ridden a horse on the wrong lead in a turn can testify to the choppy, rough, irregular movement that the wrong lead produces. Just as a person riding a motorcycle into a hard turn leans into the turn to maintain balance and counteract centrifugal force, a dog that starts going into a turn on the wrong lead instinctively will tend to shift to the correct lead to put the weight back toward the inside of the turn.

Certainly counter-balancing centrifugal force in a turn affects which lead a dog chooses, but so do some other factors. A horse tends to have a dominant lead—he'll favor one lead over the other. In teaching a horse to accept a rider, the trainer often has to teach the horse to shift leads, using a combination of pressure points, rein pressure, and even verbal cues. Are there also dogs that are lead dominant? Certainly there are. In executing rear crosses, these dogs always spin the wrong way or turn wide in only one direction while turning cleanly and tightly the other way. Although dogs tend to have dominant leads, most tend to shift leads more easily than other animals, perhaps in part because dogs were originally predators that had to be able to react and turn quickly to keep up with unpredictable, fleeing prey. Some dogs even shift leads when they are moving in a straight line, a skill that comes in handy when tackling a staggered line of jumps in an angled configuration with variable spacing. The dog that can *autoshift* leads to accommodate challenges of spacing and jump angles will jump better even while his handler remains on one side of the jump line.

A third factor influences a dog's choice of lead. If you watch a dog and handler run with the handler on the right side, you will see the dog mostly on the right lead. If the handler switches sides, the dog will be mostly on a left lead. Thus, the handler's position is part of what communicates to the dog which lead to choose. This is why we in agility say that the dog will always turn toward the handler. The dog's lead is already set for the side that the handler is on.

Consideration of lead and lead changes is vital in handling jumps on courses. The sequence in **Figure 5-1** presents two jumps at 90° to each other with the handler on the inside of the right turn. Given the physics of leads, with the handler on the right, the dog will be on a right lead on approach to the turn and will maintain the right lead throughout the turn. As the dog lifts off the ground, he maintains the right lead in front configuration, the right foreleg leaving the ground before the left. Watch though when the dog lands. Even though the right (lead) leg is in front, the left foreleg lands slightly before the right. It's a small but detectable difference. Landing with the left forefoot just before the right foot *sets the turn*, so that the dog can maintain the right lead into the turn. An analogy would be a runner who wants to turn right but actually plants the left foot first to set the turn.

Figure 5-1. In a turn to the right, a dog on a right lead will maintain his right lead, although his left foreleg lands first off the jump, to set the turn.

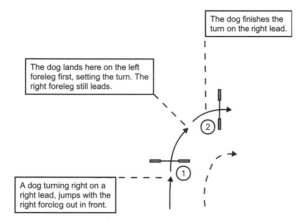

The dog finishes the turn on the right lead.

The dog lands here on the left foreleg first, setting the turn. The right foreleg still leads.

A dog turning right on a right lead, jumps with the right foreleg out in front.

When the handler is on the inside of his dog in a turn, the dog doesn't have to change leads. However, when the handler has to change sides to accommodate the twists and turns of an agility course, how does the handler get the dog to change leads? One way is to use a verbal directional cue. If the handler has taught his dog verbal directionals, the handler can tell the dog which way to go. This ability enables the dog to set the proper lead and to turn in the correct direction. If the handler can't tell the dog *Left* or *Right*, he can still get the dog on the correct lead by using the body language of handler maneuvers like front or rear crosses.

In **Figure 5–2**, the handler is on the dog's right and wants to turn the dog to the left, away from the expected direction. Between jumps #2 and #3, the handler can execute a rear cross. As the handler moves from the right to the left, an attentive dog should change leads from right to left just before he has to jump to allow a smooth landing and a nice, simple transition to the turn at jump #4. A handler who can't—or doesn't—cross behind early enough runs into the kind of trouble illustrated in **Figure 5–3**. The closer the handler gets to the obstacle he needs to cross behind (jump #3, in this case), the less likely the dog will get the cue early enough to change to a left lead. Instead, the dog most likely will take off and land on a right lead, resulting, for most dogs—and especially green agility dogs—in a spin to the right or a *Border Collie donut*. The quickest way for the dog to get back on track is to continue spinning right a full 270° to get to the left jump, but that solution presents a real potential for the dog to backjump #3. Even if the dog doesn't backjump #3, the turn in the wrong direction will waste time.

If the handler cues the rear cross slightly earlier, the dog might pick up the signal to change leads as he begins to land. Instead of landing on a right lead, the dog may try to change to a left lead without enough time to complete the shift. The dog will end up *neutralizing* the leads—landing with both feet at the same time, as in Figure 5–3. This solution makes it easier for the dog to shift to a left lead but exacts a price. Since the dog lands with both feet going straight ahead, he must first continue forward in a straight line before he can start to set the lead to the left. Therefore, the dog's turn will be wide. While more efficient than the donut spin, the dog that neutralizes his lead still loses time on this sequence, perhaps more so because he'll likely have to turn back to complete jump #4 from right to left.

If the dog picks up the lead-shift cue just after taking off, he may attempt to change from the right lead to the left lead in the air, executing what is known as a *flying lead change*. While a flying lead change sets the dog for the correct lead early enough for a proper landing, attempting the adjustment in mid-air is tricky. When the dog shifts leads, the left foreleg comes forward and the right drops back to the trail position, which is fine if the dog's front legs have cleared the jump bar. At roughly the same time, however, the dog shifts his rear legs as well, and they are likely still on the takeoff side of the bar. As he brings the trail leg forward, it may knock the bar, as in Figure 5–3. The physics of this fault are simple: When the dog jumped, he had planned the spacing to accommodate a right-lead jump. With the unplanned lead shift, the left hind leg comes forward prematurely for the jump arc spacing and hits the bar near the top of the arc.

Figure 5-2. Properly executing a rear cross requires giving the dog notice and time to change leads.

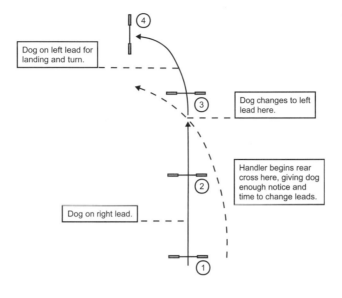

Dog on left lead for landing and turn.

Dog changes to left lead here.

Handler begins rear cross here, giving dog enough notice and time to change leads.

Dog on right lead.

Figure 5-3. A poorly executed rear cross produces spins in the wrong direction, knocked jump bars, or wide turns because the dog does not have enough notice or time to change leads.

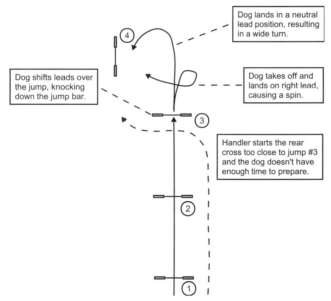

Dog lands in a neutral lead position, resulting in a wide turn.

Dog shifts leads over the jump, knocking down the jump bar.

Dog takes off and lands on right lead, causing a spin.

Handler starts the rear cross too close to jump #3 and the dog doesn't have enough time to prepare.

To avoid the problems shown in Figure 5-3, the handler needs to be proactive. He needs to start the rear cross early enough so that the dog can start shifting leads before he leaves the ground. Another solution is for the handler to give a verbal cue to shift leads so that his dog can start setting up the lead shift well before jumping. Both of these cues are *takeoff-side* cues that give the dog ample time to shift leads before he needs to, on the takeoff side of the obstacle.

One reason that front crosses are gaining again in popularity is that a well-timed, properly executed front cross is a much more proactive maneuver than a rear cross. That's because the handler is out in front of the dog, indicating the new direction before, or just as, the dog takes off at a jump. This signal gives the dog time to sort out lead shifts before he lands. A poorly timed front cross will cause the dog to turn wider than a poorly timed rear cross, however, because a poorly timed front cross will provide a landing-side cue, giving the dog information after the fact. It gives the dog no information on the lead change and, in fact, indicates that the direction is straight ahead, not a turn. This is why handlers need to take care in planning front and rear crosses. A good rule of thumb is: If you have to race your dog just to get to the front cross, then a rear cross, however awkward, is likely the better choice.

6   Concepts of Course Analysis

Now that we have a good working knowledge of terms, conditions, and challenges in agility, we can start applying what we have learned. Let's start by examining some basic guidelines for analyzing courses.

Study the Course Beforehand

While examining the course beforehand is not always possible, usually a trial offers exhibitors printed copies of courses. Course copies enable the handler to take a look at the course and get a feel for its flow and pace before he walks it. If the course seems choppy on paper, for example, chances are the actual course will be as well. Studying the course diagram also allows a handler to start looking for trouble spots in handler positioning, challenges, or other areas that might pose a problem. By identifying trouble spots early, the handler can spend more time figuring out what maneuvers or handling style a specific part of the course might require.

Look at the Course from the Dog's Point of View

When examining course diagrams or the actual course, if the handler hopes to get the dog the proper information in a timely fashion, it is important to look at the course in terms of how the dog sees it. Often what the handler sees is radically different from what the dog sees, in large part because the handler knows where to go. When walking the course, the handler can walk the dog's path and crouch at the dog's eye level to see what the dog sees. When looking at course diagrams, the handler can get an idea of what the dog might look at by drawing straight lines on the course, as in **Figure 6-1**, representing what the dog would be looking at if he were lined up in front of a particular obstacle.

Figure 6-1. To get a dog's perspective of a course sequence, draw a straight line from the dog's position, showing what the dog will be looking at if he is lined up in front of, or performing, an obstacle.

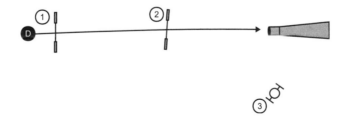

This exercise should give the handler an idea of the dog's *line of sight* on course. Then the handler can draw an optimal dog path, as in **Figure 6-2,** to show how the dog needs to move to the correct obstacle.

Figure 6-2. Draw the dog's optimal path over the path indicating the dog's perspective.

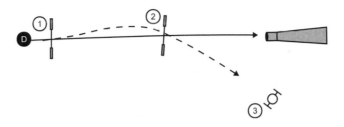

Draw the Handler's Path

On the course diagram, draw the handler's path and then sketch in the probable dog's path that would result from the planned handling, as in **Figure 6-3.** This exercise can give the handler an idea of whether his proposed path will help or hinder the dog. In this example, the proposed handling path clearly interferes with the dog's path and will probably lead to an off-course at the tunnel. To avoid the off-course and to help the dog negotiate the hazard, the handler might need to slow down his dog, change his path, or add an additional maneuver, as in **Figure 6-4.** The handler can then add notes on exactly what he needs to do.

Figure 6-3. Draw the planned handler path, then the dog's probable path as a result of the handling choice.

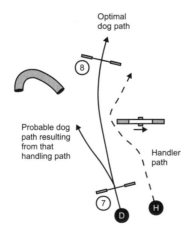

Figure 6-4. Consider potential changes in the handler path to aid the dog in moving to the correct obstacle. In this case, the front cross option might work for a slow dog and a fast handler who can get there in time.

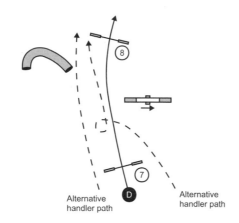

Think of a Course in Terms of Sequences

Rather than thinking of a course as a series of individual obstacles, it is to the handler's advantage if he learns to think of the course as a series of sequences, as in **Figure 6-5**. In this example, instead of thinking of this course as eight individual obstacles, it is much easier to grasp two sequences: one sequence consisting of three jumps to the teeter and a second sequence of three jumps in an arc to the A-frame. By concentrating on sequences rather than individual obstacles, the handler frees up his mind for strategizing how to handle a particular sequence instead of just trying to remember which obstacle his dog is supposed to do next.

Figure 6-5. When you look at this diagram, do you see eight individual obstacles or two sequences of four obstacles each?

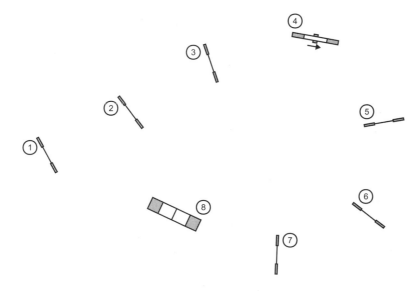

Practice the Course in the Walk-Through

Once the handler has identified what he needs to do on course, he should use the walk-through to practice handling maneuvers and commands. Practicing the run puts the handler's mind at rest because he's "been there, done that." It also gives the handler an idea of how the run will look and identifies any additional problems that he might not have noticed while examining the course diagram. After looking at the course diagram, but before the real walk-through, some handlers even practice a mental course walk-through to get a head start on the actual walk-through. After the walk-through, many handlers also practice the course mentally, going through step by step how they plan to move, where they plan to cross, and when and what commands they plan to give. In essence, they picture their perfect run.

7

Course Analysis Practice

Now that we know how to go about looking at a course we're going to run, let's examine half a dozen sequences and analyze what we need to do. Keep in mind that all the ways discussed to handle a sequence will work to one extent or another. There is no such thing as a "best" handling option. You have to decide based on the type of dog you have, his speed, your speed, and so on, which handling strategy will work best for you in a particular situation. Remember: The more efficient or more forgiving strategies will be better choices overall.

Note: Although the obstacles in each sequence are numbered consecutively from #1 through the last obstacle, the assumption is that these sequences would occur in the *middle* of a course rather than at the start—unless a start line is specifically noted. Therefore they do not offer the handler the option of a lead-out advantage.

Sequence 1

Figure 7-1. Sequence 1

At first glance, the sequence in **Figure 7-1** appears easy. But, take a closer look:

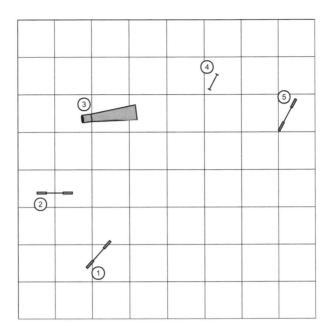

- The chute is a *blind* obstacle, meaning that the dog will not be able to see the next obstacle in sequence until he emerges from the chute. Moreover, since most dogs tend to pull the chute toward the handler rather than driving straight through it, and since the handler will probably be on the right of the chute in this sequence, the dog will likely initially turn right—away from the #4 jump.

- Since the jump after the chute (#4) is a nonwinged jump, it is harder for the dog to see, even more so because this jump is also angled.

- Since the second jump after the chute (#5) is a winged jump, set square to the chute, it is more dominant in appearance than the #4 nonwinged jump. Therefore, it will tend to draw the dog forward and around the #4 nonwinged jump.

The faster the dog and the farther ahead of the handler he moves, the harder it will be to get the dog out to the nonwinged jump. As the dog turns right barreling out of the chute, the slower handler will draw the dog even further right. As a result, the dog typically either makes a wide, loopy turn to the nonwinged jump or completely runs by it, as shown in **Figure 7-2**. For a handler who can keep up with his dog but needs to run with him to each obstacle for the dog to perform it, there is a possibility that the dog and handler may collide. The handler has to get ahead of his dog and move to the left to get the dog to turn cleanly to the #4 nonwinged jump as he exits the chute. To get ahead, the handler must send his dog over jumps #1 and #2 to the chute, as in **Figure 7-3,** and then take a short cut to the exit of the chute so that he is ready to push the dog to the nonwinged jump.

Figure 7-2. The solid line is the probable path of a dog whose handler (dotted line) lags behind or runs with his dog to each obstacle. The dog will turn right as he exits the chute and the handler will have difficulty pushing the dog out to jump #4.

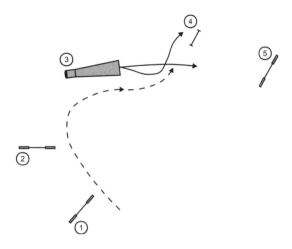

Figure 7-3. A handler who can send his dog to the chute and take the short cut to jump #4 is at a distinct advantage for managing this sequence.

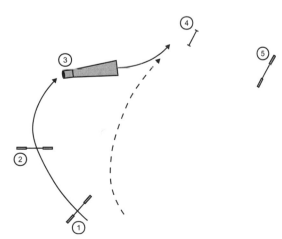

Although a slower dog allows the handler to get to the chute exit in time, the dog still can earn a refusal at the nonwinged jump if he doesn't focus on the jump until the handler pushes him toward it. The handler needs to get far enough in front of the dog so that he can start pushing left to jump #4 as soon as the dog emerges from the chute.

Another way of tackling this sequence is for the handler to cross behind the chute to pull the dog to the left and toward the nonwinged jump, as in **Figure 7-4**. This strategy requires a technically more perfect handler, however. If the handler executes a dramatic rear cross, he can easily pull his dog out of the chute. Even if the cross is successful, the dog will turn left out of the chute toward his handler and will need a push toward the #4 jump. Since the #4 jump is also to the left, this maneuver will give the handler an advantage *if* he can get to the end of the chute in time to push his dog. Then, unless the handler can outrun the dog to the #5 jump, he'll have to cross behind jump #4 to get his dog turned to #5. The drawbacks of this strategy outweigh the advantages.

Figure 7-4. A rear cross at the chute may get the dog to the #4 jump, but it may pull the dog off the chute as well. If the cross does succeed, the handler is then faced with the necessity of another rear cross at jump #4 to get the dog to #5.

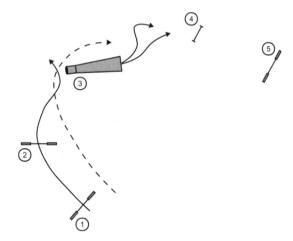

Another option is for the handler to execute a front or blind cross at the chute exit, then cross behind the #4 nonwinged jump to pull the dog back to the right, as illustrated in **Figure 7-5.** This difficult strategy not only requires that the handler get in front of the dog to perform the front cross, but that he find the nonwinged jump quickly and turn to it before the dog goes around it.

Figure 7-5. A front or blind cross, followed by a rear cross, can work well with a fast handler who can get to the crossing point.

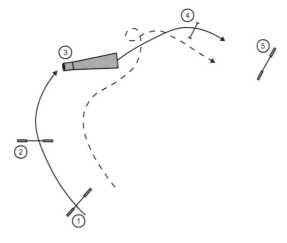

Sequence 2

The sequence in **Figure 7-6** presents several obstacle discriminations.

Figure 7-6. Sequence 2.

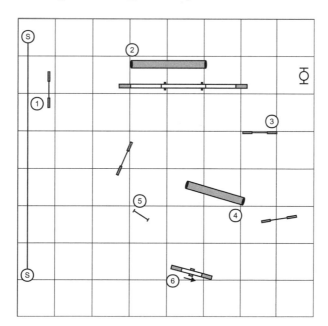

Suppose the handler sets up his dog on the start line so that he is square to the first jump. The handler then leads out to block the dogwalk, pushes the dog to the #2 tunnel, and runs between the dogwalk and tunnel to pick up his dog at the tunnel exit. Next, the handler calls his dog to him and runs with his dog on his left to the #3 jump and then to the #4 tunnel. At the tunnel exit, the handler pushes the dog to the #5 nonwinged jump and crosses behind him to turn the dog to the teeter.

In an ideal world this handling plan would work, and indeed in the real world it can work. However, this sequence offers great potential for disaster. Consider the opening obstacle discrimination. If the handler sets his dog square to the #1 jump, the dog will be looking directly at the dogwalk, not the tunnel. If the dog ignores the handler, even a lead-out and strong push to the tunnel may not counter the dog's focus and drive to the dogwalk. Getting the dog from the tunnel exit to jump #3 presents an even bigger problem since the dogwalk blocks a timely turn to jump #3 and the off-course tire beckons, as in **Figure 7-7**. To get his dog turned past the dogwalk and away from the tire, the handler needs to keep moving forward while at the same time keeping the dog close at his left side and handler-focused.

Figure 7-7. Taking the path between the dogwalk and the tunnel pushes the dog toward the off-course tire.

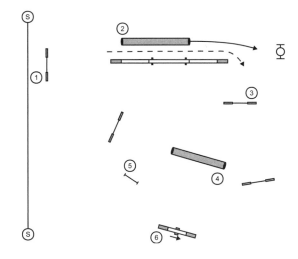

The problems with approaching jump #3 don't end there. Once the handler has cleared the dogwalk, he then will be blocking the dog's path to the #3 jump. If the handler moves out of the way to the left, he'll push the dog off the jump. Therefore, he'll need to move right to draw the dog toward jump #3, as in **Figure 7-8**, but this step will aim his dog toward the wrong tunnel entrance. Although the handler can probably avoid the off-course tunnel entrance, the dog's path will be loopy or erratic.

Figure 7-8. As the handler pushes out around the dogwalk to head toward #3, he is in the dog's path to #3 and can easily push his dog off the jump. Moving to the right to draw the dog to jump #3 will aim the dog toward the wrong tunnel entrance, resulting in a loopy path to get the dog to #4.

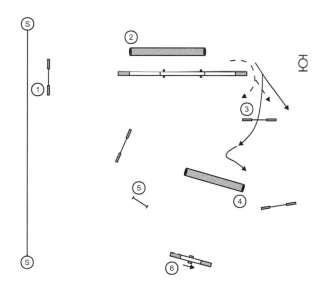

Once the handler gets his dog into the tunnel at #4, the turn to the #5 jump presents a challenge. A straight pipe tunnel, where the dog can see right through to the end, tends to lengthen a dog's stride—no matter what his speed—more than a curved tunnel. The dog will see the off-course jump long before he emerges from the tunnel. A handler who races the length of the tunnel to get in front to control his dog's exit often signals that the dog is supposed to barrel toward the off-course jump (remember the power of the handler's forward motion).

Given these factors, if the dog exits the tunnel even with or ahead of his handler, one of the four scenarios illustrated in **Figure 7-9** likely will result:

1)   The dog takes the off-course jump.

2)   The handler and dog collide.

3)   The dog runs to the outside of the #5 jump.

4)   The handler manages to get his dog away from the off-course jump, but the dog is still focusing to the right, away from the #5 nonwinged jump. A fast dog that doesn't have enough time to focus on the #5 jump will earn a refusal. A slower dog may avoid the refusal but likely will turn wide to the #5 jump.

Figure 7-9. If the dog exits the tunnel even with or ahead of his handler, an off-course, refusal, collision, or wide turn to #5 will be the probable result.

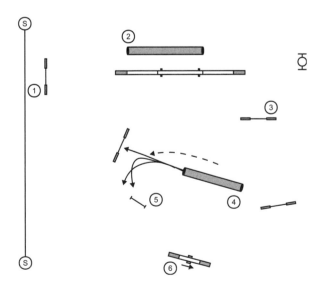

If the handler elects to cross at the tunnel entrance, using either a front or a rear cross, the dog may take the off-course winged jump near the tunnel entrance. Additionally, since a rear cross will be of the dramatic type, its drastic nature may pull the dog off or even out of the tunnel, as in **Figure 7-10**. To avoid such a reaction, the handler will need to delay his rear cross until his dog is well inside the tunnel, but doing so means that the handler may not get close enough to the #5 jump to direct his dog over the obstacle. If the dog realizes that the handler has crossed behind him at the tunnel entrance, the dog will take a sharp left as he exits to look for his handler. If the dog doesn't realize that the handler has crossed, he'll turn right as he exits the tunnel. In either case, the handler will need to correct his dog's focus instantly to get the #5 jump.

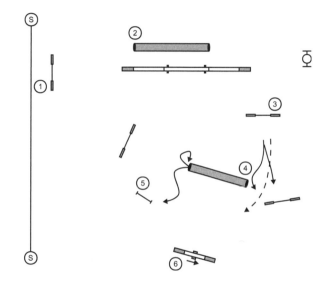

Figure 7-10. A rear cross at the #4 tunnel entrance can cause the dog to take the off-course jump near the tunnel entrance, pull the dog off the tunnel, cause him to spin in the wrong direction as he exits, or turn sharply left at the exit, which creates a wide turn to #5.

There are easier options for handling this sequence. If the handler sets up his dog to the right behind jump #1, as in **Figure 7-11**, then the dog can see the tunnel. In addition, if the handler gives a *Get Out* directional command, he can push the dog out to the #2 tunnel while staying on the right side of the dogwalk, as in **Figure 7-12**.

Figure 7-11. Instead of setting up the dog straight on to jump #1, set him to the right so that the #2 tunnel is in his line of sight.

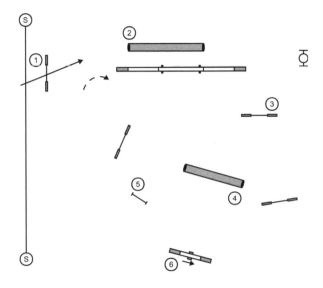

Figure 7-12. Using a "Get Out" command and layering the dogwalk puts the handler in a better position for guiding his dog to the #4 tunnel.

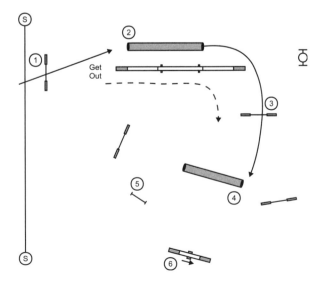

By layering the dogwalk, the handler can better control the dog's path out of the tunnel because the dogwalk is no longer in the handler's way. If the dog exits the tunnel faster than expected, the handler can signal the dog and physically start turning to the right toward jump #3. Besides giving the handler more flexibility in giving the dog correct information in a timely fashion, layering the dogwalk reduces the off-course potential of the tire because the handler doesn't have to drive toward it to get around the dogwalk. Finally, layering the dogwalk puts the handler in a better position to go from jump #3 to the tunnel at #4 since the handler won't be caught behind the #3 jump.

As for the turn to the #5 jump, if the handler can cross to the other side of the #4 tunnel before the dog comes out, it will be a lot easier to turn the dog left to the #5 nonwinged jump. To guarantee that the handler can get to the other side of the tunnel before the dog emerges, the handler will need to take an on-course lead-out and send his dog to the #4 tunnel with a *Get Out* command, as in **Figure 7-13.** The *Get Out* allows the handler to move away from the dog to pick him up at the tunnel exit. A minor drawback of this strategy is that the unmarked jump at the tunnel entrance presents a potential off-course. However, since most dogs will more readily head for a tunnel than a jump, and since the tunnel is the more dominant obstacle of the two, chances are that the dog will head for the #4 tunnel.

Figure 7-13. Using a "Get Out" to send the dog to the #4 tunnel followed by a front or blind cross at the tunnel exit sets up the dog correctly for jump #5.

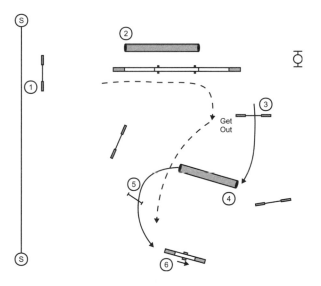

Once the handler sends the dog out to the tunnel, the handler can cut the corner and execute a blind or a front cross at the tunnel exit. The advantage of the blind cross is that acceleration after the cross is immediate, so the off-course jump presents far less of a threat than it does to the handler who is slow coming off the front cross and potentially can still push his dog over the wrong jump. In either case, the handler doesn't have to wait until the dog emerges to set him up for jump #5. Instead, as soon as the dog dives into the tunnel, the handler can start his cross. Since the tunnel is straight, the dog can see his handler move from right to left. On exiting, the dog should automatically turn in the new direction and ignore the off-course jump.

The drawback of these choices is that they depend on the handler being able both to send his dog away and to work his dog at a distance. The handler who has trained these skills, however, gains more flexibility to proactively set up his position on the course to better aid his dog.

Sequence 3

In **Figure 7-14**, the sequence runs from an A-frame to a pinwheel of jumps to a set of weave poles. The assumption is that the handler can start on either side of the A-frame. The sequence presents two potential off-courses:

- Coming off the A-frame when the dog is faced with two jumps (#2 and #4).

- After the last jump of the pinwheel (#4) when the dog could opt for the off-course A-frame as easily as for the weave poles.

Figure 7-14. Sequence 3.

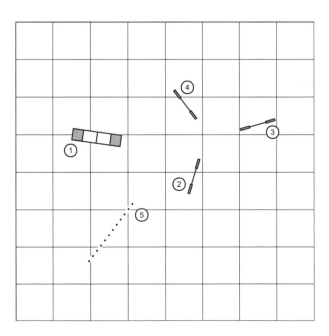

If the handler starts on the left side of the A-frame, getting his dog around the pinwheel on his right should be easy, especially since the handler will avoid having to change sides at the start of the pinwheel. A potential problem arises if the dog comes off the contact before the handler gets to the end of the A-frame, as in **Figure 7-15**. Since the handler is on his left, the dog may bear left to take the off-course #4 jump. Although possible, this off-course isn't likely because #2, the correct jump, is more directly in front of the dog than the off-course jump. The dog would have to have run significantly in front of his handler to make an uncontrolled left turn toward the off-course jump.

Figure 7-15. If the handler is on the left and gets too far behind his dog at the A-frame, he may cause his dog to bear left toward the off-course #4 jump.

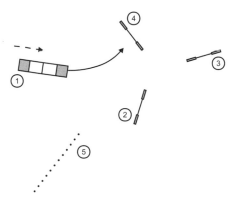

To get his dog to the weaves, the handler has four choices:

- As in **Figure 7-16**, he can cross in front of the last jump in the pinwheel to turn the dog to the weaves and away from the A-frame. Such a maneuver also takes the dog's focus off the A-frame and puts it on the handler. The disadvantage of the front cross here is that, if the handler steps forward instead of to the right, he can push the dog over the #2 jump again.

Figure 7-16. A front cross at jump #4 turns the dog toward the handler and away from the beckoning A-frame.

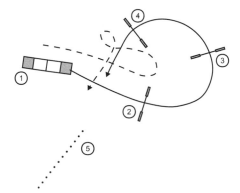

- He can keep the dog on his right side throughout the pinwheel, in which case he must get his dog's attention and keep it until the dog has *finished* making the turn toward the weaves—otherwise, he risks his dog taking the A-frame, as in **Figure 7-17**.

Figure 7-17. If the handler keeps the dog on his right for the entire pinwheel, after the last jump, he must get his dog's attention and keep it until the dog has finished making the turn toward the weaves—otherwise, he'll push his dog toward the off-course A-frame.

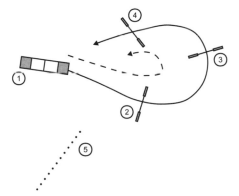

- He can go into the pocket and layer the #2 jump, as in **Figure 7-18**. This maneuver gets the handler out of the way more so that he is less likely to push the dog onto the A-frame. The drawbacks are that the handler has to be able to layer a jump, and since he hasn't changed the dog's angle over the #4 jump, the dog could still take the off-course A-frame. However, the off-course potential is low since the handler won't step into the dog and change his path.

Figure 7-18. Layering the #2 jump makes the turn to the weaves easier and lessens the off-course potential of the A-frame.

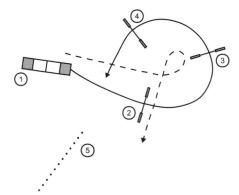

- He can change the angle between #3 and #4 by setting a V and passing on either side of the #2 jump, as in **Figure 7-19.** The V-set changes the dog's path over #4 so that he gets a better angle of approach to the weaves and minimizes the potential for taking the A-frame. The disadvantage is that it can put the handler farther behind the dog.

Figure 7-19. A V-set between #3 and #4 takes the A-frame out of view and aims the dog straight at the weaves.

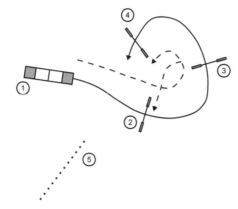

Working on the right side of the A-frame, the handler is more certain to get the dog to the #2 jump. But then he has to cross behind the #2 jump, as in **Figure 7-20,** to get the dog to turn left to #3.

Figure 7-20. A handler on the right side of the A-frame can execute a rear cross on the takeoff side of the #2 jump to turn his dog around the pinwheel.

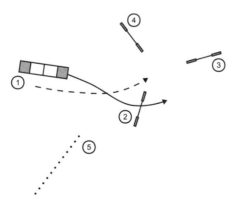

To execute this cross, the handler needs to have the dog out in front or settle for a landing-side rear cross, as in **Figure 7-21**. The latter maneuver will widen the turn to #3 and may put the handler behind if he plans to cross in front at #4. After the rear cross at #2, the handler can elect any of the choices above to handle the rest of the pinwheel.

Figure 7-21. If the dog isn't driving ahead at #2 for a takeoff-side rear cross, the handler can execute a landing-side rear cross. Then, however, the dog will turn wide to #3, and the handler may have to scramble to get to #4 if he's planning a front cross to steer his dog to the weaves.

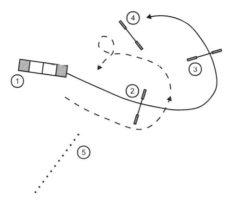

Another option is for the handler to cross in front of the downside of the A-frame and eliminate the problem of a rear cross altogether, as in **Figure 7-22**. To execute the front cross, the handler must be able to outrun the dog to the end of the A-frame or the dog must be trained to wait for a release on the down contact.

Figure 7-22. A front cross at the down ramp of the A-frame eliminates potential problems with rear crosses at #2, but to execute a front cross, the handler must be able to beat the dog to the end of the obstacle or the dog must be trained to wait on the contact.

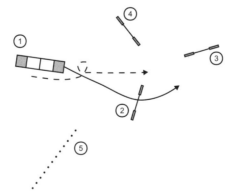

The only advantage of working the right side of the A-frame is if the dog is way ahead of the handler.

In handling the turn to the weaves, the front cross, the V-set, and the layering of #2 are all about equally efficient. The choice then depends on where the course goes after the weave poles. If the course bears right after the weaves, then the front cross and on-side weaves are a better option. If the course veers left, then the V-set and layering for off-side weaves are better options. Between the V-set and layering, if the next obstacle is farther away than normal, then layering of #2 is the better choice since it puts the handler farther down the course. With the V-set, the handler has to go into the pocket between #3 and #4, which puts him farther behind. If the handler needs to cover a lot of ground, he may have a harder time catching up with his dog.

Sequence 4

The obvious problem presented in the sequence in **Figure 7-23** is the discrimination between the A-frame and the tunnel, exacerbated by the orientation of the jump sequence that precedes it. Because of the generous spacing between jumps #1 through #3, the dog will increase speed over the gentle arc of jumps. This acceleration ensures he'll not only land further off jump #3 before the A-frame but also that he will enter the turn to the A-frame with more speed. Both factors guarantee a wider turn toward the obstacle discrimination. What the handler does, or fails to do, to set up his dog for the discrimination will determine the team's success or failure.

Figure 7-23. Sequence 4.

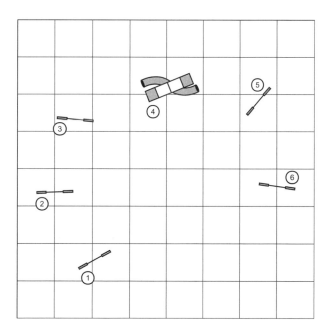

Suppose the handler comes into the sequence with the dog on his left. He commands his dog to jump. He waits until the dog clears jump #3 before calling the wide-turning dog off the tunnel. Because the handler is concerned about pushing in toward the A-frame until the dog's focus is off the tunnel and on the A-frame, he also hangs back a bit, as in **Figure 7-24**. Once he turns the dog away from the tunnel, the handler can direct the dog to the A-frame. This scenario may still set up the dog to jump wide and head straight toward the tunnel. If the handler does successfully call the dog away from the tunnel, because the handler is hanging back, the dog may also pull off the A-frame and earn a handler-induced refusal. Moreover, if the handler tries to rush in to get the dog on the A-frame, he can inadvertently push the dog back toward the tunnel.

Figure 7-24. Hanging back may help the handler turn his dog away from the off-course tunnel, but it also might pull the dog away from the A-frame.

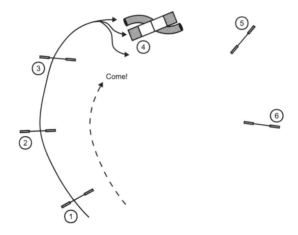

The key to avoiding the off-course tunnel is adjusting the approach to and the landing from jump #3. There are three suitable solutions for avoiding the tunnel:

- The handler can execute a front cross between jump #3 and the A-frame, as shown in **Figure 7-25**. A front cross here allows the handler to keep the dog handler-focused and keep his mind off the beckoning tunnel. To be successful, the handler needs to be in front of the dog or else risk a wide turn or even drawing his dog into the tunnel. Also, since the dog needs to go right to jump #5 after the A-frame, the handler will either have to cross in front again after the A-frame or immediately cross behind the dog as he ascends the A-frame. An immediate rear cross behind the A-frame not only may slow down the dog but also may pull him off the A-frame.

Figure 7-25. If the handler opts for a front cross after jump #3, he'll need to change sides again to turn his dog toward #5. He can either immediately cross behind his dog as the dog is ascending the A-frame or he can go around the far side of the A-frame and cross in front of the dog at the down ramp.

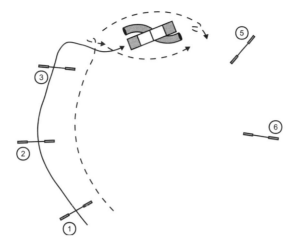

- The handler can set a V between jumps #2 and #3. This lines up the dog more toward the A-frame and takes the tunnel out of play, as in **Figure 7-26**. This maneuver also eliminates the need for the handler to change sides. The drawback of this choice is that if the handler can't keep up with his dog or can't get a lead-out in the jumping sequence, there is no way to set the V and the dog then takes the path to the tunnel. The V-set choice might work better for a somewhat slower dog that is responsive to his handler since a V-set bleeds off the dog's speed less than the front cross would here.

Figure 7-26. Performing a V-set eliminates the need to change sides.

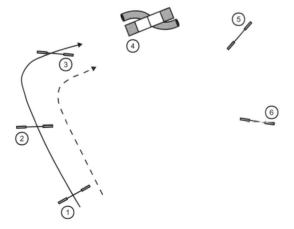

- The handler can turn the dog faster on the landing side of jump #3 by executing a reverse flow pivot (RFP) right after the jump, as in **Figure 7-27.** An RFP slows the dog's forward motion to the tunnel and brings him in tighter to the handler. Once the handler has the dog's focus, he pivots back in the original direction to get the dog on the A-frame. A handler with a fast, driven dog or a handler who is far behind the dog will find it easier to use the RFP because it elicits a better response at a distance. The drastic nature of the RFP makes this maneuver less suitable for slower or easily deflated dogs.

Figure 7-27. A handler can use an RFP to tighten the dog's landing-side turn, pulling him quickly away from the tunnel.

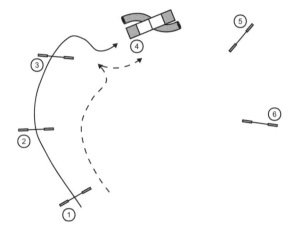

In the three options outlined, the RFP is a landing-side cue, the V-set is a takeoff-side cue, and the front cross can be either, depending on where the handler executes the cross in relation to the dog. The front cross and the V-set work better for handlers who can keep up with their dogs, while the RFP works better for handlers who cannot get a fast dog to gear down over a jump at a distance.

Sequence 5

The sequence in **Figure 7–28** presents a serpentine with a two-jump lead-in and a tunnel at the end. Assuming that the handler starts on the left of the lead-in jumps and aims the dog straight at the #3 jump, the handler has to call the dog back over the #4 jump, push to #5, and then on to the tunnel.

Figure 7-28. Sequence 5.

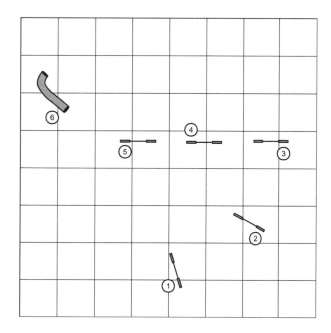

The resulting path, shown in **Figure 7–29**, is wide and loopy for the following reasons:

1.   The dog jumps #3 jump from left to right, instead of from right to left, which puts the #4 jump behind and to the left of him instead of in front of him.

2.   Since the handler has to hold back to keep his dog from running past #4, the handler ends up behind and to the left of the dog going to #5. The handler's position initially makes the dog look in the wrong direction before he heads to the #5 jump, so once again the turn is wide.

Figure 7-29. If the handler doesn't try to control his dog's approach to the serpentine, a wide, loopy path will be the likely result.

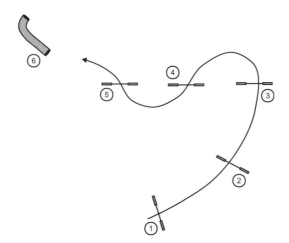

Consequently, the dog runs a much greater distance than what the judge might measure and racks up a longer course time. In addition, the handler has taken no steps to avoid run-bys and consequent refusal penalties. Clearly, the handler needs to do something besides just calling his dog to turn.

The solution lies in controlling the approach to the #3 jump:

- The handler can cross in front of the #4 jump, as in **Figure 7-30**, to tighten the turn and to place him in the proper position for the eventual turn to the tunnel. As usual, the drawback is that the handler needs to be able get there to perform the front cross. If the handler gets behind the dog during the two-jump lead-in, the front cross will be late and the turn after #3 will be wide. However, the handler still should be able to control and tighten the turn to #5, as in **Figure 7-31**.

Figure 7-30. The handler can use a front cross at jump #3 to tighten the dog's turn to #4.

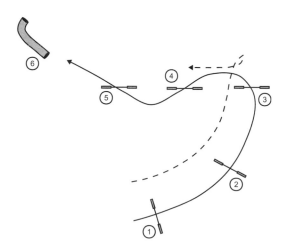

Figure 7-31. If the handler gets behind the dog and the front cross is late or poorly executed, it will make the dog's first turn wide, but the handler will still be in a position to tighten the turn to #5.

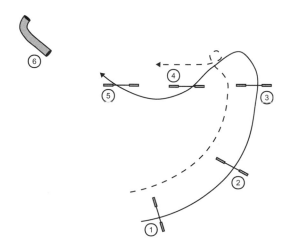

- The handler can set a V between #2 and #3, as in **Figure 7-32.** The handler keeps the dog on the right throughout the sequence. This strategy sets up the proper angle to enter the serpentine. Properly executed, the V-set will allow both turns to be tight because the obstacles following the V-set are in front of the dog rather than behind him. The dog can now move directly to the next obstacle and doesn't need to scan to find it. The drawback is that although the handler doesn't need to be right next to his dog to set the V, he does need to get close to the dog to be successful. If he gets in a race with the dog to the V-point, the handler may push the dog by the #3 jump and earn a refusal. If the dog is far ahead in the serpentine, the handler needs to cross behind quickly between #4 and #5 and push through the gap to the tunnel to turn his dog, as in **Figure 7-33.** Otherwise, the dog will likely arc right off the #5 jump and turn away from the tunnel, requiring that the handler turn him back.

Figure 7-32. A V-set aligns the dog nicely for a smooth, fast execution of the serpentine.

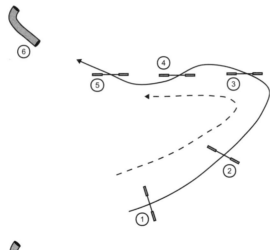

Figure 7-33. A handler who gets behind his dog after the V-set will need to cross behind the dog between jumps #4 and #5 and then keep moving forward to prevent the dog from turning too far to the right after #5 and missing the tunnel entry.

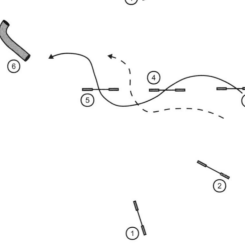

- The handler can execute blind or front crosses after every jump in the serpentine, as in **Figure 7-34**. This maneuver puts the dog in extreme handler-focus. In essence, the dog follows the handler to the next obstacle, which is a way to keep a slower dog constantly moving. The disadvantage is that the handler must be able to stay in front of the dog throughout, so the dog needs to be slow enough or the handler fast enough for this plan to work. Moreover, it's easy for the handler performing blind crosses, or a series of rapid-fire front crosses, to lose track of his dog and whether the dog actually took the next jump or just ran by it. While the front/blind cross variation works successfully on serpentines, it should be reserved for slower, more distractible dogs.

Figure 7-34. Executing two blind crosses gets the dog through the serpentine nicely, if the handler doesn't lose track of his dog.

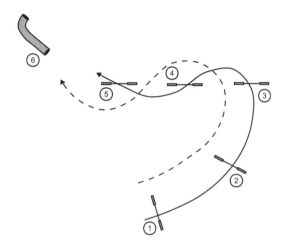

Sequence 6

For the sequence in **Figure 7-35**, if you assume the handler is on the right side of the dog and teeter, all he needs to do is turn right to take the panel jump and then push to the weaves. But, take a closer look. With the handler on the right, his anticipated path is close to the end of the down ramp of the teeter, which puts him directly behind the panel jump and forces him to dash around the right jump wing. The handler's corrective maneuver pulls the dog to the right, so that the handler then has to push back to the left to get the dog into the weaves. The unmarked jump adjacent to the weaves and directly in front of the panel jump exacerbates the problem. Since the panel jump is a blind obstacle, meaning the dog can't see what is on the other side until he clears the jump, he'll register the dummy jump first, especially when his handler dashes around the right wing of the panel jump. So this increases the dog's desire to bear right. If there were plenty of space between the panel and weaves, the handler could correct the dog's path by pushing him into the weaves. But here the distance between the obstacles is barely 18'—and remember, the dog initially will be heading right.

Figure 7-35. Sequence 6.

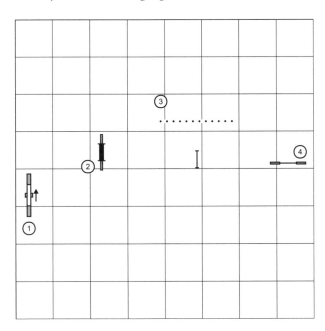

If the dog is looking at the handler or at the dummy jump, or he cannot see the weaves soon enough because the panel blocks his view, he is likely to miss the weave entry and earn a refusal, as in **Figure 7-36**. To handle this sequence this way, the handler must be much faster than his dog and the dog has to be relatively laid back. For other teams, handlers need to figure different strategies.

Figure 7-36. Handling on the right side can easily cause a refusal at the weave poles because the dog is likely to focus on the unmarked jump, and the handler must run around the wing of the panel jump. Both of these factors pull the dog to the right away from the weave poles. There is very little room between the obstacles for the handler to correct the dog's path for a successful weave entry.

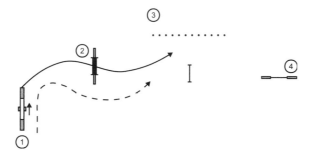

First, since the dog doesn't know that the weaves are to the left of the panel jump, the handler must indicate that the dog needs to move left. Second, since the panel will block the handler's movement if he goes to the right, he instead should move to the left of the panel and draw his dog left. There are two choices here for getting the dog into the weaves efficiently:

- The handler can cross behind the panel jump to turn the dog to the left, as in **Figure 7-37**. The risk of the rear cross is that if the dog doesn't pick up the direction change early enough, he may still run a straight line initially, creating a harder approach to the weaves.

Figure 7-37. One option to get the dog turning toward the weaves over the panel jump is to execute a rear cross behind the panel jump.

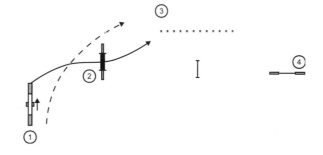

- The handler can cross in front of the dog at the down ramp of the teeter so that the dog is on his right for the weave entry, as in **Figure 7-38.** This strategy draws the dog left after the panel, eases his entry into the weaves since he is already turning toward the obstacle, and takes the unmarked jump out of play. Additionally, the approach angle to the weaves is softer so that the dog has an easier time with it. If the handler doesn't complete the front cross before the dog gets off the teeter, however, the turn from the teeter to the panel can be wide or loopy, as in **Figure 7-39.**

Figure 7-38. Crossing in front of the dog at the down ramp of the teeter puts the handler in a good position to aim his dog directly at the weave poles.

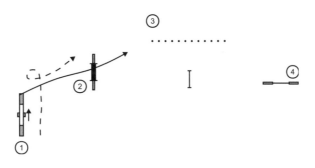

Figure 7-39. If the front cross is late because the dog gets off the teeter before the handler gets into position, it will push the dog wide and away from the panel, causing a loopy turn.

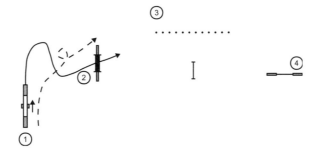

All things considered, the front cross at the downside of the teeter is a better choice for most dogs since it gives them information on the turn earlier.

Once the dog is in the weaves, regardless of which of those two options the handler used, the handler needs to cross again to get on the right side of the dog and set up the turn to #4. The handler can cross behind the weaves or he can execute a front cross after the weaves, or he can push the dog to the right after the dog completes the weaves, as in **Figure 7-40**. Of the three options, the rear cross is probably the most efficient since it allows the dog to immediately understand where he is going next. The front cross tends to slow the dog and keep him handler-focused until the handler turns in the new direction. A push to the #4 jump probably produces the widest turn since initially the dog is looking and heading in the wrong direction.

Figure 7-40. To turn his dog to the right after the weaves for jump #4, the handler can cross behind the dog before the weaves, cross in front of the dog after the weaves, or push the dog toward jump #4 at the weave exit.

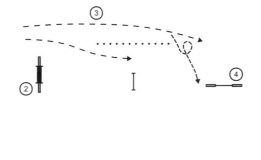

8

Putting it All Together

We now have some terms and concepts that give us a useful frame of reference in analyzing sequences. Before applying these concepts to formulate a strategy for running an entire course, we need to discuss the concept of running a course as a series of *sequences* as opposed to running it from *obstacle to obstacle*. By definition, running a course from obstacle to obstacle involves the handler concentrating only on the next obstacle in the sequence. In essence, the handler works the dog one obstacle at a time; instead of running a 20-obstacle course, the handler runs 20 one-obstacle courses. This way of running courses can earn the dog and handler a qualifying score but limits the speed of the dog to the speed of the handler since the dog doesn't move ahead much.

The obstacle-by-obstacle approach also makes it hard to work at any distance since the dog, cueing off his handler, doesn't look any further than the next obstacle. This problem is particularly apparent when a fast dog runs with a slow, lagging handler. The dog takes an obstacle and then either turns, spinning back to the handler, or "head-checks" (turns his head toward the handler) before going on to the next obstacle, producing a broken or choppy run. Because the dog is constantly checking his forward motion—tapping the brakes after every obstacle—his course time typically is slower. These teams have problems with courses requiring difficult handling maneuvers since the handler always seems to be out of position, and the dog is too handler focused.

By contrast, a handler that runs in sequence-to-sequence mode tends to have faster course times since his dog looks further ahead than just to the next obstacle. The dog has a longer "focal length" that enables him to see a line of obstacles. Given the proper cues, the dog takes the correct obstacle, even though the handler may be far behind. The dog drives forward without any spins or head-checks, generating increased speed. The runs tend to look smoother on simpler sequences, and the handler doesn't seem to work as hard at getting the dog through even a challenging course because he always seems to be in the right position. That's because the handler doesn't have to baby-sit the dog on every obstacle so can position himself at points where his efforts might be more critical, like an obstacle discrimination challenge. These dogs are obstacle focused, that is, they don't always wait for the handler to give them direction but try to think further ahead than the next obstacle.

When analyzing a course, it's convenient and easy to break it down into sequences where the flow tends to be disrupted or change directions (see **Figure 8–1**). For example, if you have a straight line of three jumps to a fourth jump set on a sharp turn to the right, the handler needs to think of a strategy to change the dog's path so that the dog doesn't run around the fourth jump.

Figure 8-1. In this course, you can see breaks in the flow between #2-#3, #5-#6, #7-#8, #9-#10, and #10-#11, with a minor change from #3-#5.

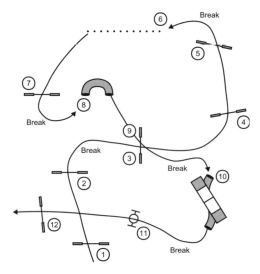

Points in the course where you can break up sequences include

- Changes of direction greater than 30°

- Obstacle discrimination problems

- Sharp turns toward the handler

- Spots where the handler is required to change sides

In considering the Standard course in **Figure 8-2**, keep in mind that all the handling options described *will* work. Which you choose depends on three factors:

1. The speed of the dog and handler.

2. The efficiency (or competitive edge) that each option provides.

3. How forgiving each option is—that is, if something goes wrong, how easy it is to fix and to get back on track. This is known as the *recoverability factor*.

Figure 8-2. A Standard agility course.

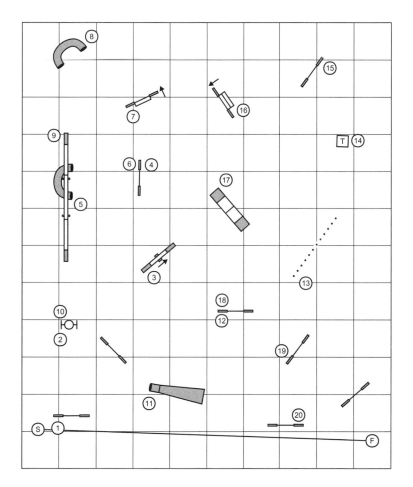

Sequence #1–#3

The opening sequence in **Figure 8-3** offers potential problems right off the start line. Lining up the dog straight with the #1 jump going to the tire also lines him up straight for the off-course dogwalk instead of the teeter at #3. Handling this start-line challenge depends on the speed of the dog, the speed of the handler, the side the handler chooses to work his dog, and whether the handler can make the dog wait at the start line.

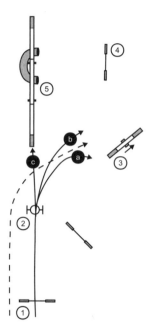

Figure 8-3. Various scenarios await the handler who starts on the left of jump #1 and tries to outrun his dog to push him to the teeter. The dog may make too shallow a turn and either awkwardly loop toward the teeter (a), or run by the teeter (b), or even slip by the handler onto the dogwalk (c).

Starting With the Dog on the Right

If the handler opts to start to the left of jump #1 with the dog on his right side, he has several choices:

- Outrun and push

- Lead out and push

- Rear cross

Outrun and Push—The handler can try to outrun his dog to push him to the #3 teeter as shown in Figure 8-3 and then keep the dog on the right for an easier turn to jump #4. To successfully execute this strategy, the handler needs to be faster, and often much faster, than his dog. In addition, the dog needs to understand that the handler is trying to push him onto the teeter. While an occasional handler can probably perform this feat, these are the typical results of trying to outrace the dog:

- The dog outruns the handler and heads for the dogwalk or runs into the handler.

- The dog turns wide if the handler can't push hard and fast enough to turn him.

- The dog turns hard, but not quite hard enough, causing a difficult approach to the teeter and possibly a missed up contact.

Several factors can cause this high failure percentage (the dog taking an off-course, earning a refusal, or missing the contact) of pushing the dog:

- The handler on the left side of the course trying to outrace his dog draws attention to obstacles either in front of the dog or on the left side of the course.

- The teeter is on the right of the dog (the *away side*) and thus is difficult to see, let alone reach. This gives the dog little time to react to a change in direction.

- The tire acts as a "picture frame," bracketing the dogwalk and drawing attention to it. This setup, called *obstacle framing*, effectively screens the teeter from the dog's direct view.

- The handler can attempt to push the dog into the turn only on the landing side of the tire, which is late when asking for a change of direction.

Handlers should also be aware that pushing the dog early in the course will tend to slow him down on other parts of the course since the dog won't know when the handler might cut him off next. Thus, always anticipating the unexpected, the dog will slow down.

Lead Out and Push—A slower handler could conceivably lead out, but any lead-out needs to be absolutely reliable. If the dog breaks the stay and starts before the handler is ready, the potential results are much the same as in Figure 8-3.

Rear Cross—If the handler chooses to cross behind the tire as shown in **Figure 8-4**, the placement of the unmarked dummy jump will force him to cross behind his dog late, when the dog is almost on top of the tire.

Figure 8-4. Similar to the situation shown in Figure 8-3, a handler who starts on the left and crosses behind his dog is likely to create an awkward approach to the teeter, a run-out, or an off-course onto the dogwalk.

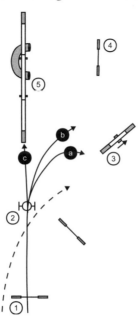

As shown in **Figure 8-5**, this delay in the rear cross pushes the dog further out in a straight-line direction than is desirable. A fast dog could be through the tire before the handler even has a chance to complete the cross. Usually, the handler also has to call his dog in to get him close enough to the teeter to take it.

Figure 8-5. The ideal rear cross path would run the handler into the dummy jump. The only possible handling path for the rear cross means performing the cross late, a delay that will push the dog further out in a straight line than desired.

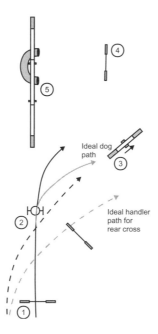

Thus, while the above choices for the handler starting with the dog on his right will work, they aren't the most efficient ways of handling this sequence and pose a host of problems.

Starting With the Dog on the Left

Three options for the handler who chooses to start from the right of jump #1 with the dog on his left side are worth considering:

- Lead-out pivot

- Lead out and call

- V-set

Lead-Out Pivot—If the dog has a steady stay at the start, the handler may opt for a lead-out pivot shown in **Figure 8-6**. The handler stands beyond the tire, facing the dogwalk, looking over his left shoulder, and signaling the dog with his left arm while he calls the dog. As the dog approaches the tire, the handler pivots 270° toward the dog and turns to the teeter, pushing the dog to the teeter. The dog is now on the handler's right side, which makes the turn to jump #4 easier. An advantage of the lead-out pivot is that it allows the handler to block the dog from the dogwalk, although some dogs will still get by the block.

Figure 8-6. A lead-out pivot can be effective if the handler turns hard and executes it with precise timing. If he turns too early, he'll pull the dog off the tire; too late, and the dog will land long and turn wide.

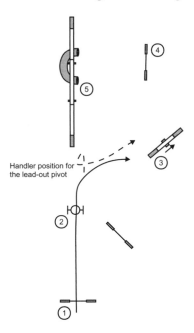

The lead-out pivot will work a good percentage of the time and is more efficient than handling with the dog on the right, but there are some drawbacks.

- The tire still frames the dogwalk, so the dog may go for the dogwalk despite the handler's body language to turn.

- The handler needs to turn hard to position the dog to take the teeter rather than running around it.

- If the handler pivots too quickly, his dog may bump the tire hard or even turn away from the tire. If the obstacle #2 were a jump rather than the tire, the dog could easily drop the bar.

- If the handler waits for the dog to clear the tire before he pivots and cues his dog (on the landing side of the tire), the dog will land long and turn wide. The handler needs to communicate to the dog to turn *before* he jumps so, ideally, the dog will collect his stride when jumping the tire. Otherwise, the dog will turn wide on landing.

Still, despite its disadvantages, the lead-out pivot can be a good way to turn and control the dog in this challenging opening sequence.

Lead Out and Call—Starting with the dog on his left as in **Figure 8-7**, the handler can run with the dog or lead out and call his dog to the teeter. These options offer the handler distinct advantages:

- The handler doesn't have to count on beating his dog around the turn to push the dog to the teeter.

- If the dog breaks the stay and starts moving, the handler can still get the dog turned easily enough.

Figure 8-7. Starting with the dog on the left, the handler can call his dog to the teeter relatively easily, although the dogwalk—framed through the tire—still beckons and could induce an off-course or an awkward approach to the teeter.

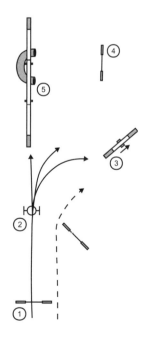

These options are not, however, without potential disadvantages.

- If the handler lines up the dog straight with the tire, the dogwalk still beckons to his dog since it's framed by the tire.

- A wide turn and awkward approach to the teeter are still potential problems, but less so since the handler is on the side the dog needs to turn toward.

- Although the unmarked dummy jump still causes the handler to delay his turn, when the dog turns wide, the handler can over-turn and slide right to get the dog rotated toward the teeter as shown in **Figure 8-8**. This emergency maneuver, however, will make it harder for the handler to get to the teeter and then into position to turn the dog to the #4 jump.

Figure 8-8. The location of the dummy jump makes a timely signal to turn right difficult. The handler may need to compensate by over-turning and sliding to the right after the dummy jump to get his dog to the teeter.

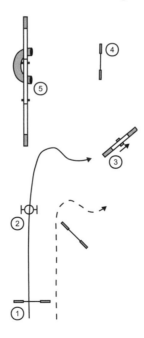

V-Set—To set a V between the #1 jump and the #2 tire, the handler sets up his dog slightly offset to the right, pointing left. The handler takes only a slight lead-out (if any) and pushes the dog left as illustrated in **Figure 8-9**. Before the handler reaches the tire, he turns right so that the dog slices the tire at a left-to-right angle and continues to the teeter. A rear cross before the teeter or a front cross after the teeter will put the handler in position to handle #4 through #6.

Figure 8-9. A V-set at the tire takes the dogwalk out of view and aims the dog directly at the teeter. A rear cross before the teeter or a front cross after will put the handler in position to handle #4 through #6. The V-set is an excellent choice for a handler who can push his dog into the V and cross either before or after the teeter.

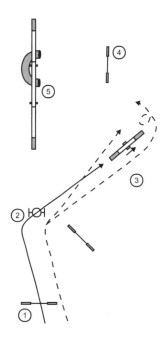

The handler and dog gain a definite advantage by setting a V:

- By offsetting his dog at the start line, the handler not only takes the dogwalk out of play but, equally important, he also puts the teeter in view from the takeoff side of the tire and thus cues the dog much earlier.

- Since the handler adjusts the dog's angle before the take-off point at the tire, on landing the dog has a shorter, quicker path to the teeter.

- Since the handler is now offset as well, the unmarked jump is largely out of the way, which gives the handler a straighter path to the teeter. Because of the more direct path to the teeter, the handler wastes no time trying to over-rotate or slide right to turn his dog to the teeter and, instead, can concentrate on either crossing behind at the up ramp or in front at the down ramp of the teeter to set up for jump #4.

There are a few disadvantages to the V-set in this situation:

- If the dog doesn't push to the left to set the V, he will jump straight through the tire with a resulting fractured turn.

- If the handler pushes too far left, the dog may go around the tire. Because the tire has limited clearance, a large dog may be at a disadvantage getting through.

- The handler has to be able to either cross behind or in front of a contact obstacle.

Given the choices available, the V-set and the lead-out pivot are the most viable options in handling this opening sequence. Which option the handler selects depends on evaluating speed, efficiency, and recoverability as they apply to each member of the team.

Sequence #4–#6

The key to handling this sequence is controlling the dog's angle over jump #4. An uncontrolled turn to the tunnel at #5 can result in an off-course, a refusal, or a wide, loopy turn.

Dog on the Right

Ideally, the handler needs to be on the left side of the teeter (dog on the right) so that he is on the inside of the turn to #4 and #5. The lead-out pivot puts the handler on the left side of the teeter and so does a V-set followed by a cross behind or in front of the teeter. From the left side of the teeter, the handler has several options for handling #4 to #6:

- Pulling the dog

- Front cross

- V-set

- Counter rotation

Pulling the Dog—The handler can keep the dog on the right over jump #4 and then pull the dog toward the tunnel at #5. However, the dog's arc from the teeter to the #4 jump aims him toward the wrong tunnel opening as shown in **Figure 8-10**. If the handler moves toward the tunnel, he can easily send his dog into the wrong end. If the handler stops and calls his dog off the wrong opening, he will probably have to over-turn to get the dog aimed at the correct opening. Even then, the dog may slide by the opening, incurring a refusal. If the dog does turn off the wrong opening and go into the correct one, the turn will be wide and loopy. The handler will also be left in a poor position for handling the next sequence. Thus, an uncontrolled send to jump #4 and a simple pull to the left off the jump could cause significant problems.

Figure 8-10. The handler can simply keep the dog on the right and pull to get the dog to #5. However, this uncontrolled turn can cause significant problems: an off-course, a refusal, or a wide, loopy turn.

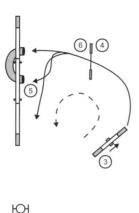

Front Cross—If the handler crosses in front of the dog after #4 as in **Figure 8-11**, he gains several advantages.

- He puts the dog in handler focus, slowing him down enough to sharpen the turn and making it less likely that the dog will take the wrong tunnel opening.

- He puts the dog on his left side, allowing him to push the dog out slightly to get the correct tunnel entrance.

- He gains more control of the dog's turn than he would by simply trying to call the dog to the correct entrance.

- He puts himself in a better position to handle the next sequence.

Figure 8-11. A front cross at #4 turns the dog toward the correct tunnel entry and puts him in handler focus so he is less likely to take the wrong end of the tunnel. The dog is still jumping toward the wrong tunnel entrance, however, and a poorly executed front cross could push him to the off-course tunnel entry.

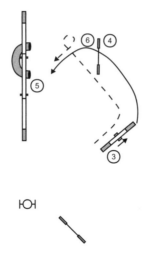

But there are potential pitfalls as well:

- If the handler fails to get to the pivot point in time to perform the front cross, the dog can still turn wide.

- When racing to get in front of the dog to cross, the handler can push the dog into the wrong tunnel entrance—although the handler is facing his dog, he is actually backing up toward the wrong tunnel opening and signaling the dog to continue in the wrong direction.

- The dog will tend to turn wide since he is still jumping #4 from left to right, toward the wrong end of the tunnel.

For the dog to get a clean turn to the correct tunnel opening, the handler needs to start turning the dog on the takeoff side of jump #4. This is a challenging maneuver, since the straight line from the teeter to the jump takes the dog in the wrong direction. Changing the dog's jumping angle requires the handler to get a lead-out advantage. Since obstacle #3 is a contact, most handlers will stay close to the teeter to make sure the dog hits the contact rather than attempt a lead-out while the dog is on the teeter. This delay can cause any front cross to break down, leading to the problems previously described.

V-set—Setting a V between the #3 teeter and the #4 jump as in **Figure 8-12**, sets the angle from #4 to #5 cleanly to the tunnel's left opening. It also provides the following benefits:

- The V-set essentially eliminates the turn from #4 to #5 since the handler has turned the dog before he ever jumped #4.

- It takes the wrong tunnel entrance out of the dog's view on the takeoff side of jump #4.

- The dog isn't in handler focus for as long here as with the front cross and therefore should move faster on this part of the sequence.

Figure 8-12. A V-set focuses the dog on the correct tunnel entry before he even takes jump #4. However, this maneuver also puts the dog on the handler's right, forcing the handler to make a dramatic rear cross to get to the tunnel exit.

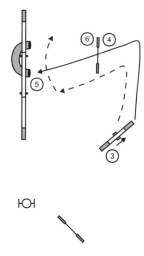

These are the disadvantages of the V-set:

- If the dog cuts in front of the handler and takes the jump at #4 while the handler is moving perpendicular to it, the handler can be in a worse position for the turn.

- As with the V-set for the opening sequence, the handler can push the dog around the jump, especially if #4 were a nonwinged jump.

- The V-set puts the dog on the handler's right side so that the handler will have to perform a dramatic rear cross to get in position for the next sequence. If the dog is behind the handler, the rear cross will be harder to execute and present the potential for pulling the dog off the tunnel.

Counter-Rotation: The handler can move parallel to jump #4 well past the teeter, and then execute a counter-rotation to change sides and the dog's direction as in **Figure 8-13**.

Figure 8-13. A counter-rotation is an effective but roundabout way to get the dog aimed at the correct tunnel entrance, but it's also a tricky maneuver. The handler has to get to the counter-rotation pivot point in time and clear the right wing of the #4 jump to avoid sending his dog into the wrong end of the tunnel.

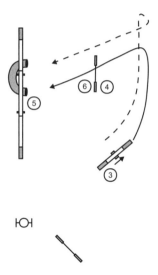

Executed properly, this counter-rotation will aim the dog from right to left over jump #4, heading directly toward the correct tunnel entrance. While this maneuver is more reliable than the rear cross, it is a roundabout way to get the dog to the proper tunnel entry. If the handler doesn't go far enough before performing the counter-rotation, he'll have to run around the right wing of the jump, which will pull the dog to the right initially and, consequently, toward the wrong tunnel opening. To remedy that situation, the handler will have to try to beat the dog around the corner of the jump to push the dog into the correct tunnel opening (not likely), or cross behind the dog to turn him. All the crosses and changes of side may slow down the dog and focus him on the handler so much that he misses the correct tunnel opening.

Between the front-cross and the V-set, which is the better option here? For the dog that can be sent a short distance to an obstacle, the V-set would probably be the better choice since it allows the dog to maintain greater speed overall and eliminates the pressure on the handler to get in position for the front cross. For slower dogs with faster handlers, or for dogs well versed in reading the handler's body language, the front cross would be the better option. A front cross allows the handler to get closer to the exit of the tunnel to help turn his dog so that the handler can set up faster for the next obstacle.

Once the dog is in the tunnel, the handler can move to either side of the exit to get the dog to the #6 jump, his choice determined by where the dog needs to go next.

Dog on the Left

If the handler can't cross behind or in front of the dog on the teeter and ends up on the right side of the teeter with his dog on the left, he can still help the dog take the correct tunnel opening, despite being in a poor position. There are two potential handling options from the right side of the teeter:

- Rear cross

- Reverse V-set

Rear Cross—The handler can move straight ahead from the teeter to the #4 jump and cross behind the dog as in **Figure 8-14.** This will turn the dog left toward the tunnel, but there is no guarantee how far left the dog will turn. Since the incorrect entrance of the tunnel is the first one the dog sees, there is a good likelihood that he will choose it.

Figure 8-14. Crossing behind jump #4 turns the dog left, but how far? It may not control the dog's angle over the jump as much as the handler needs for a clean entry to the tunnel at #5.

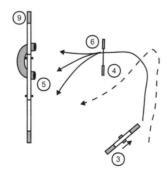

Reverse V-Set—The handler can use a reverse-V-set from the teeter as in **Figure 8-15**. Just as in the counter-rotation option, the handler pulls the dog out past the teeter. But instead of crossing in front of the dog, the handler lets the dog drift ahead to the V-point and then crosses behind him and sets the direction to the correct tunnel entry. All the usual problems of the V-set as well as the reverse V-set come into play. Of the options for the handler stuck on the right side at the teeter, however, this one has the best potential for success. It also is a little more forgiving than the rear cross because it allows the handler some control, although the sequence may be choppy.

Figure 8-15. A reverse V-set, with the handler crossing behind his dog, is a more controllable and more forgiving option than the rear cross, but it's a challenging maneuver to master.

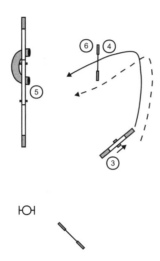

Sequence #6—#9

At first glance, the sequence from #6 to #9 seems straightforward. All the dog has to do is turn left over jump #6, take the double to the #8 tunnel, and head straight to the dogwalk. But it's not so simple.

- If the dog takes a straight path out of the #5 tunnel, the first thing he will see besides the #6 jump is the A-frame, beckoning him off-course as in **Figure 8-16**.

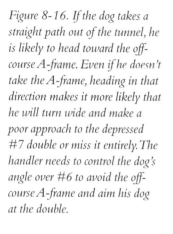

Figure 8-16. If the dog takes a straight path out of the tunnel, he is likely to head toward the off-course A-frame. Even if he doesn't take the A-frame, heading in that direction makes it more likely that he will turn wide and make a poor approach to the depressed #7 double or miss it entirely. The handler needs to control the dog's angle over #6 to avoid the off-course A-frame and aim his dog at the double.

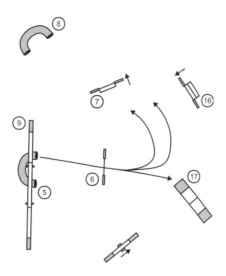

- Even if the dog doesn't take the A-frame, he's likely to turn wide to the double, which will add time and distance to his run, if he doesn't turn so wide that he misses the double completely.

- If the dog turns wide to the double, he'll tend to slice it from right to left and aim toward the wrong opening of the #8 tunnel as in **Figure 8-17**.

Figure 8-17. If the dog turns wide to the double, he'll probably jump it from right to left, which will aim him at the wrong tunnel entry. With a tighter turn to the double, he's more likely to head straight for the correct entry.

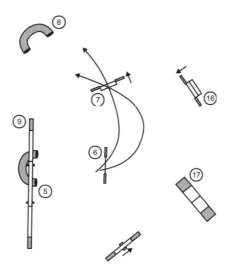

- Another potential pitfall for a dog that slices the double at an acute angle is that he may knock the double bar. **Figure 8-18** illustrates how slicing a jump increases the chances of knocking a bar. This is especially true for smaller dogs because, at an acute angle, the spread width that the dog jumps can be wider than the maximum permitted width.

Figure 8-18. When slicing a jump, a dog is jumping a greater depth (B) than he would if he headed straight over the jump (A). For that reason, slicing double or triple jumps at an acute angle poses risks of knocking bars, especially for little dogs, because the difference in jump depth is proportionately greater than for larger dogs.

To avoid these problems, the handler needs to carefully set up how his dog jumps both the #6 jump and the #7 double.

Dog on the Left

Rear cross—If the dog is on the handler's left after he completes the tunnel at #5, the handler only has one option: to cross behind the dog as he takes jump #6 as shown in **Figure 8-19**. Providing the dog is paying attention, the rear cross will turn him left. Once again with the rear cross, though, the handler may not be able to control the radius of the dog's turn. The dog potentially can turn wide as easily as he can turn tight. Since the handler starts on the outside (right) of the turn (left), it's probable that the dog will turn wide and may even fly by the double. Once the dog starts drifting by the double, the handler will have a tough time getting him back over it.

Figure 8-19. A rear cross at the #6 jump will turn the dog left, but since you can't control the radius of the turn, steering him toward the double at #7 may still be a challenge.

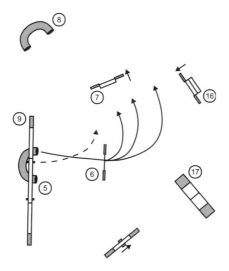

Dog on the Right

If the handler picks up his dog at the tunnel exit on his right side, he'll signal his dog that a turn is imminent and the dog's turn is likely to be tighter because the handler is on the inside of the turn. Depending on what option the handler chose for the previous sequence, he may need to execute a rear cross or a front cross to get into position on the far side of the #5 tunnel.

If the dog is on the handler's right as he exits the tunnel at #5, there are three handling options for the #6 to #9 sequence:

- Pull
- V-Set
- Deceleration

Pull—To communicate an upcoming left turn, the handler can simply call the dog and pull as in **Figure 8-20**. Since the handler is on the inside (left) of the required turn (left), the dog theoretically should turn tighter. In reality, this handler-side turn will probably be only somewhat tighter because a simple pull left does not provide that much control of the dog's arc. Still, the handler-side turn is a better choice than the rear cross.

Figure 8-20. If the handler picks up his dog at the tunnel exit on his right side, he'll signal his dog that a turn is imminent. The dog's turn is likely to be tighter because the handler is on the inside of the turn. Still, because the handler can't control the dog's arc, the dog may jump the #7 double at an angle that aims him at the wrong #8 tunnel entry.

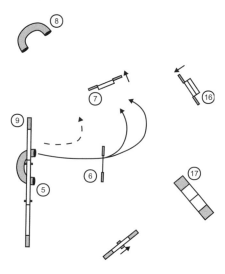

V-Set—By setting a V before jump #6 as in **Figure 8-21**, the handler alters the dog's angle over jump #6, making the approach to the double more direct and taking the A-frame out of view. This strategy will make the turn tighter to the double since it is a takeoff-side turn—that is, the dog is turning before he takes the jump. Because the dog will be set more squarely over the double, it also sets the angle for the correct tunnel entrance at #8.

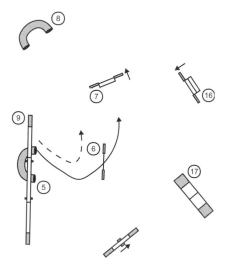

Figure 8-21. Setting a V over the #6 jump takes the off-course A-frame out of view and steers the dog toward the double.

Deceleration—The handler slows the dog on the approach to jump #6 so that the dog will shorten his stride and land closer to #6, making the turn to the double tighter. This will also set up the dog more squarely over #7, which sets the angle for the correct tunnel entrance at #8. The drawbacks of deceleration are that the dog's pace will be slower so that he will lose time, and he will get a long, hard look at the A-frame for a potential off-course.

Again, the V-set seems to be one of the better choices for speed, ease of execution, and recoverability.

Once the dog has entered the tunnel at #8, the dogwalk should be easy to reach.

Sequence #9—#11

After the dogwalk, the course heads straight through the tire and hooks left to the chute. The challenge is to determine at what point the handler is going to turn left toward the chute. The placement of the dummy jump complicates the turn.

Dog on the Left

There is only one option for handling this sequence with the dog on the left, and it requires that the handler first cross to the right side of the dogwalk at the ascent.

Rear cross—After the dogwalk, the handler crosses behind the tire as in **Figure 8-22**. This works fine in theory. The problem is that there is no way to control the radius of the dog's turn. If the dog turns wide, he will aim directly for the chute. If he turns tighter, however, he may slip between the unmarked jump and the chute. If he turns tighter yet, he could take an off-course over the dummy jump. Clearly, this maneuver will be difficult to execute correctly, and the potential for recoverability is small.

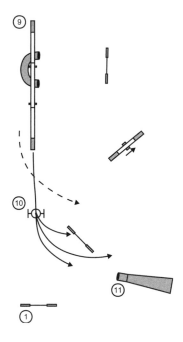

Figure 8-22. Crossing behind the dog at the tire and layering the dummy jump may turn the dog to the chute, if he turns wide enough. But controlling the dog's turn is not a given. If he turns tight, he'll earn either an off-course over the dummy jump or a run-out.

Dog on the Right

Assuming the dog is on the handler's right side, there are four options for handling #9 to #11:

- Pull
- Layering
- V-Set
- Front Cross

Pull—The placement of the dummy jump complicates matters for the handler who tries to pull the dog to the chute. When does the handler make his turn to the left? If the handler pushes past the tire and then tries to turn, he can run into the dummy jump. If the handler waits until he has cleared the dummy jump as in **Figure 8-23**, he risks pushing his dog off-course over jump #1 unless he keeps the dog's attention around the entire turn. Putting the dog into handler focus in this manner will slow down the dog.

Figure 8-23. If the handler goes into the pocket between the tire and the #1 jump, the potential for an off-course over #1 is greater. The handler opting for this strategy will have to keep his dog's attention throughout the turn to the chute.

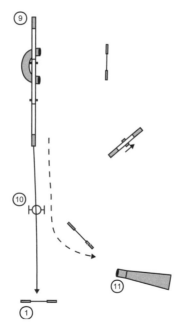

Layering—If the handler layers the unmarked jump as in **Figure 8-24,** he will avoid pushing the dog off-course over the #1 jump. Why?

•   By the time the dog lands off the tire, the unmarked jump is to his left and starting to drop behind him. Therefore, it would take extra effort to turn and take the dummy jump.

•   As the handler turns, he keeps moving toward the chute, driving the dog forward *past*, rather than *at*, the unmarked jump.

•   If the dog starts heading toward the dummy jump, the handler can move toward it from the opposite side, pushing the dog away.

Figure 8-24 . Layering the dummy jump can be an effective way to get the dog into the chute. Since the handler is running past the dummy jump, the dog has less incentive to turn hard and take it.

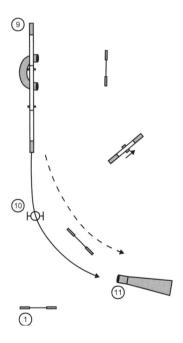

Although the dog could still take the unmarked jump, the chances for this off-course are small, especially if the handler directs his dog to *Get Out*. The layering option is safer than running into the pocket and trying to pull the dog to the chute. It is also faster since the handler doesn't have to keep the dog's focus and instead can focus the dog on an obstacle, thus generating more speed.

V-set—Another choice is to set a V between the dogwalk and the tire as in **Figure 8-25**. While this strategy should work, in reality it's more treacherous than one would think. Once again, the dummy jump interferes. Going into the pocket after the V-set will make for a faster turn to the chute, but the handler still needs to keep the dog's attention to make sure that he doesn't push his dog off-course over the #1 jump. Not much of an advantage here. If the handler elects to layer the dummy jump but gets a bit behind his dog due to the V-set, the dog can easily curl back toward the handler and take the dummy jump. At this point, the handler can do nothing to stop him. This is a case where a V-set can be detrimental to the course run.

Figure 8-25. The location of the dummy jump makes a V-set over the tire an iffy proposition at best. Stepping into the pocket (a), even slightly, can still push the dog over jump #1. Moreover, the dog can easily take the dummy jump instead of the chute, especially if his handler is behind him and opts to layer the dummy jump (b).

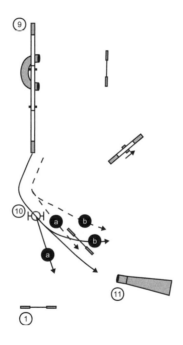

Front Cross—The handler can cross in front of the dog after the tire to slow the dog's speed through the pocket and to put himself in position to block the #1 jump as in **Figure 8-26.** The handler can then pull the dog to the chute. Of all the choices, however, the front cross probably is the least desirable for several reasons:

- If the handler executes too tight a cross, he virtually assures that he will send his dog over the dummy jump.

- The handler has to cross again so that eventually he can turn to the jump at #12.

- Since the straight-line distance to the pivot point is long, if the handler doesn't get in front of the dog to initiate the front cross, the dog can still take the #1 jump.

Figure 8-26. A front cross in tight quarters can be a risky business, if the handler can get to the pivot point at all. This maneuver necessarily puts the handler deep in the pocket where the dummy jump and the #1 jump pose strong off-course risks.

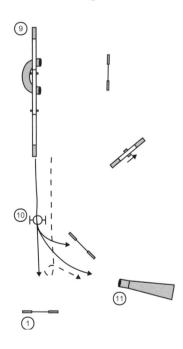

Sequence
#11–#14

In this sequence, shown in **Figure 8-27**, the turn to the #12 jump from the chute is straightforward. The only mild problems are the potential off-course at the #19 jump and the unlikely possibility that the dog will slip between the two jumps. The bigger problem is the approach from #12 to the weave poles at #13 since the dog will likely be heading straight for the A-frame.

Figure 8-27. Exiting the chute, the dog is unlikely to take an off-course, but he is likely to be heading straight for the A-frame after #12 and will need careful handling to get him into the weave poles.

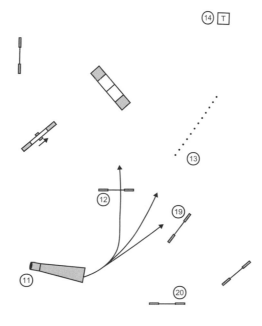

The beckoning A-frame initially pulls the dog to the wrong side of the weaves, resulting in either an incorrect entry or a loopy, time-consuming path as in **Figure 8–28**. The handler has three options to redirect his dog into the poles, all starting with the dog on his right at the chute:

- Rear cross

- Reverse V-set

- Front cross

Figure 8-28. If a handler directs his dog straight over #12, where will he end up? The handler needs to turn his dog early enough to make the weave pole entry at #13.

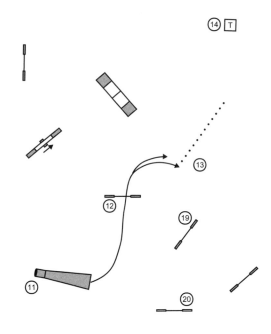

Rear Cross—Crossing behind the #12 jump without setting any angle to turn the dog back to the weaves as in **Figure 8-29**, may turn the dog too quickly. Then the handler will have to push the dog back to the weaves to get the entry, resulting in a loopy turn. A rear cross is a safe—but difficult and inefficient—way to get the dog to the weaves.

Figure 8-29. If the handler chooses to cross behind his dog at #12, he can turn the dog too sharply. This will force the handler to turn his dog back to the weaves, making for a loopy entrance.

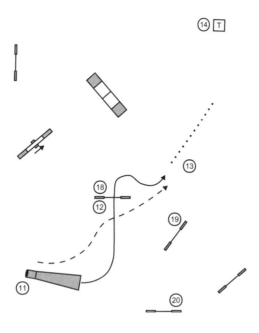

Reverse V-Set—Setting a reverse-V between the chute and the #12 jump as illustrated in **Figure 8-30**, gives the dog a better angle to the weaves and takes the A-frame out of the picture. Although posing about the same difficulty as the rear cross, the reverse-V sets the approach to the weaves much earlier, increasing the dog's chances of hitting the correct entry. The disadvantage of this maneuver is that if the dog ignores his handler's cue to turn back to set the reverse V, the handler will be in a worse position to help the dog.

Figure 8-30. Pulling the dog left in a reverse V-set and crossing behind him will aim the dog directly at the weaves, with enough notice to make a correct entry.

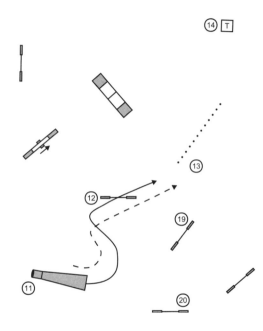

Front Cross—Executing a front cross between the chute and the #12 jump as in **Figure 8-31** offers distinct advantages:

- It puts the handler in a better position to control the turn and adjust the angle of approach to the weaves.

- It puts the handler on the dog's right for an easier, handler-side turn.

Figure 8-31. Executing a front cross between the chute and the #12 jump puts the handler in a good position to control the dog's entry to the weaves.

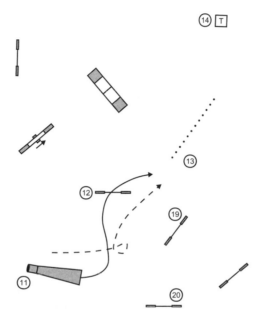

The front cross is probably the best of the three options. The limitation is that the handler has to get in front of the chute to perform the cross. Fortunately, since the dog is coming blind out of the chute, he is less likely to catch the handler sliding into the front cross.

Once in the weaves, the handler has the option of crossing behind the weaves and pulling the dog to the table or staying on the right of the weaves and pushing the dog to the table. The rear cross can be harder to execute if the dog isn't comfortable with the handler's crossing. Pushing the dog to the table can be a bit harder, but not appreciably so, since the dog will exit the weaves moving in that general direction.

Sequence #14–#17

This sequence presents a couple of tricky spots:

- The approach angle from the #15 jump to the triple is mildly depressed. This means that a dog that jumps #15 long will tend to land far from the #15 jump and turn wide to the triple as in **Figure 8-32**. Since the dog has paused on the table, however, he shouldn't have built up speed or extended his stride much, so the handler can expect a tighter turn than if the dog had been moving at full speed.

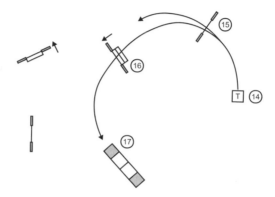

Figure 8-32. The arc from the table at #14 to the A-frame is not smooth and even; the triple is set at a slightly depressed angle, making for a wide turn by a dog that jumps long over #15.

- If the dog nevertheless turns wide to the triple, he may slice #16 at an angle, increasing the width he has to jump and the potential for dropping a bar. The generous spacing between #15 and #16, however, may allow him to straighten his approach and minimize the angle.

Once the dog has gotten to the A-frame, the handler only needs to determine which side to choose for the final sequence.

Sequence
#17–#20

Coming off the A-frame, an unchaperoned dog is likely to head for the #18 jump and land straight beyond it, making it difficult to turn to jump #19 as in **Figure 8-33**. Without the handler calling him back, the dog has moderate potential to run by #19 and earn a refusal. This strategy will lead to a loopy path to #19. The handler can choose among three options to control his dog's path off the A-frame and therefore improve the dog's turn to #19.

Figure 8-33. A dog that takes the #18 jump head on may have trouble making the turn to the #19 jump. To ease the dog's turn to #19, the handler needs to control his dog's path off the A-frame.

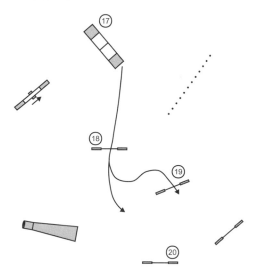

Dog on the Left

Pull—The handler can cross to the *right* side of the A-frame, putting the dog on his left side, and pull the dog to the right to set the turn. Either a rear cross between the triple and the A-frame or a front cross at the down ramp of the A-frame will put the handler on the right side of the A-frame, but both crosses present potential problems:

- A dramatic rear cross could pull the dog off the A-frame.

- If the dog leaves the contact before the handler has finished the rear cross, the dog may head toward the chute, and the handler would have a hard time avoiding a refusal.

If the handler can get in position for a front cross at the down ramp of the A-frame, he'd be better off just pushing the dog into the V-set as described below.

Dog on the Right

Working with the dog on his right side coming off the A-frame, the handler has two options for controlling the dog's turn to #19:

- Push and pull

- V-set

Push and Pull—The handler can try to drive the dog to the #18 jump and then pull to the #19 jump as in **Figure 8-34.** But this maneuver is difficult, if not impossible, with a fast dog or a slow handler. Trying to keep up with a fast dog would push the dog toward the #20 jump. To aid the dog in picking up the #19 jump, the handler needs to change the angle over #18.

Figure 8-34. A fast handler or a slow dog might manage the turn from #18 to #19 with a push out to #18 and a pull to #19, but a slow handler or fast dog would likely miss the mark.

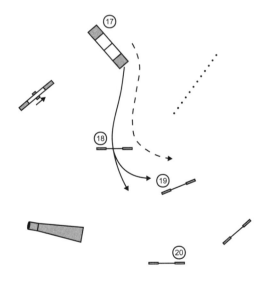

V-set—Setting a V between the A-frame and the #18 jump as in **Figure 8-35** aims the dog nicely toward #19. To get the turn set, however, the handler must get in front of, or at least even with, his dog on the down side of the A-frame. If the dog is slow or the handler is fast, this shouldn't be a problem.

Figure 8-35. If the handler can get even with his dog at the down ramp of the A-frame, he can set a V between the A-frame and #18 that should steer his dog nicely to #19.

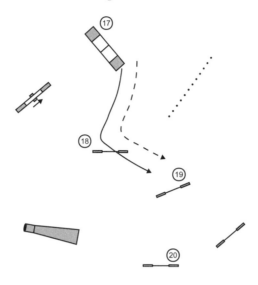

Even if the dog is fast but has a slower handler, a V-set can work. At the table, the handler can send his dog on a *Get Out* to the #15 jump, allowing the dog to take the long sweep of obstacles to the A-frame while the handler cuts the corner, as shown in **Figure 8-36.** This strategy should provide the handler enough time to get to the down ramp of the A-frame and set up for the V-set push.

Figure 8-36. For a handler whose dog will work away from him, a good option is to use a Get Out *command to send his dog on the long loop from the table to the A-frame, allowing the handler to take a shortcut to set up for the V between the A-frame and the #18 jump.*

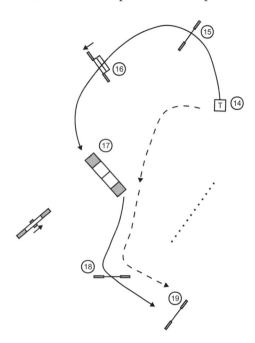

The Final Jump

Once the dog has angled over the #18 jump and is moving toward #19, the dummy jump poses a big draw for an off-course, a loopy turn, or a refusal as in **Figure 8-37**. The angle to the #20 jump, coupled with the probability that the handler will be pushing a bit to catch up with his dog, dictates that the handler do something besides simply trying to call his dog off the dummy jump. He has two alternatives:

- Reverse V-set

- Front cross

Figure 8-37. The dummy jump beckoning directly beyond #19 will make it hard for a dog that jumps straight ahead over #19 to turn to the final jump at #20. He will likely earn the off-course.

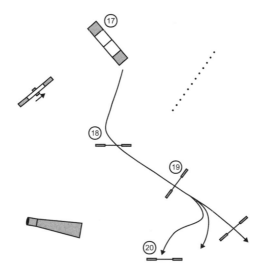

Reverse V-Set—The handler can set a reverse-V to line up the #20 jump and then cross behind #19 to finish the turn to jump #20 as shown in **Figure 8-38**.

Figure 8-38. Setting a reverse-V between #18 and #19 and crossing behind the dog should draw him to the final jump.

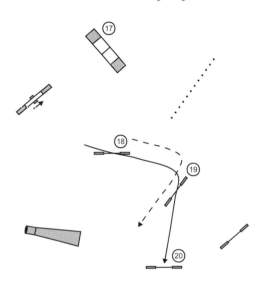

Front Cross—Another option is for the handler to cross in front between #18 and #19 as in **Figure 8-39**. If the handler elects to try a front cross here, he'll have to give up setting the V from the A-frame to jump #18. Setting the V will put him behind his dog, so he will be hard-pressed to get in position in time to execute the front cross. Performing the front cross between #19 and #20 will give up some efficiency between #18 and #19, but gain more between #19 and #20, which is probably the more critical area. The dog would have to go really wide between #18 and #19 to earn a refusal and there is also no real off-course potential here, whereas from #19 to #20 the dummy jump beckons. If one has to sacrifice efficiency on the closing sequence, the dog and handler will get into less trouble from #18 to #19 than from #19 to #20.

Figure 8-39. Crossing in front between #18 and #19 will tighten the dog's turn for a clean jump over #20, but the handler has to get to the pivot point first. That means giving up setting a V-set to control the dog's path over #18, and that may be the wiser choice here, given that #19 to #20 poses an off-course risk that #18 to #19 does not.

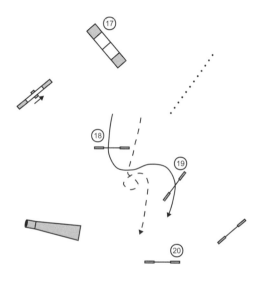

In Conclusion

Choosing from among the handling maneuvers that seemed potentially the most successful, **Figure 8-40** shows one possible handler path for this particular course. Although deciding how and what to do on a course is time-consuming at first, with practice you can learn to more easily and quickly analyze a course correctly.

Figure 8-40. Choosing from among the handling maneuvers that seemed potentially the most successful, here is one possible handler path for this particular course. You will probably come up with your own, based on your knowledge of your dog's strengths and weaknesses—and your own.

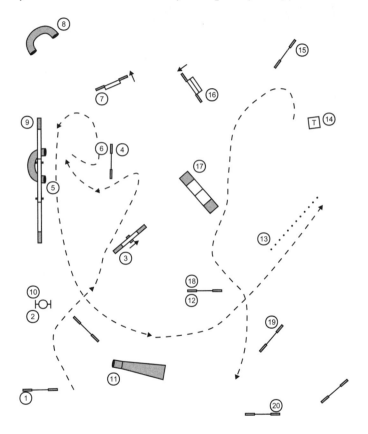

The handler plays an integral part in the successful completion of an agility course. By keeping your own and your dog's strengths and weaknesses in mind, you can approach a course realistically, By taking time to analyze a course, first on paper, then in the walkthrough, you can minimize the problems on the course run. More importantly, as you understand course analysis, you learn how to communicate with your dog more effectively through the various handling maneuvers. By understanding how dogs view the handler and how dogs move, you can make intelligent choices about which maneuvers to choose to get the best response from your dog.